Violet Harmond

Easy-7-Ingredients

MEDITERRANEAN
Diet Cookbook

FOR BEGINNERS

2000+ Days of Delightful Super Easy
Mediterranean Recipes

60-Day Meal Plan + BONUS

Table of Content

INTRODUCTION 3

What is the Mediterranean Diet? 3
A New Way of Life 3
Expectation 4
The Food Pyramid 4
20 FAQ 5

BREAKFAST 7

1. Berry Parfait Delight 8
2. Greek Yogurt Bowl 8
3. Avocado Toast Feast 8
4. Spinach Omelet Roll 8
5. Almond Chia Pudding 9
6. Mediterranean Frittata 9
7. Whole Grain Pancakes 9
8. Veggie Breakfast Wrap 9
9. Smoked Salmon Plate 10
10. Quinoa Breakfast Bowl 10
11. Tomato Basil Scramble 10
12. Cottage Cheese Delight 10
13. Olive Tapenade Toast 11
14. Mixed Berry Smoothie 11
15. Egg and Spinach Muffins 11
16. Oatmeal Banana Bowl 11
17. Tofu Scramble Plate 12
18. Mediterranean Shakshuka 12
19. Almond Butter Waffles 12
20. Walnut Raisin Porridge 12

FIRST DISHES 14

1. Mediterranean Zucchini Pasta 15
2. Tomato Basil Linguine 15
3. Garlic Spinach Spaghetti 15
4. Lemon Herb Orzo Soup 15
5. Chickpea Pasta Primavera 16
6. Greek Feta Penne 16
7. Cauliflower Alfredo Fettuccine 16
8. Mushroom Spinach Farfalle 17
9. Artichoke Lemon Linguine 17
10. Eggplant Tomato Rotini 17
11. Asparagus Pesto Spaghetti 18
12. Tuna Olive Orecchiette 18
13. Roasted Red Pepper Penne 18
14. Mediterranean Lentil Fusilli 18
15. Sundried Tomato Gemelli 19

16. Lemon Garlic Angel Hair 19
17. Broccoli Walnut Rigatoni 19
18. Zesty Shrimp Linguine 20
19. Spinach Walnut Farfalle 20
20. Mediterranean Pesto Bowls 20

MAIN COURSES 22

1. Grilled Salmon Skewers 23
2. Lemon Herb Chicken 23
3. Mediterranean Stuffed Peppers 23
4. Balsamic Glazed Pork 23
5. Shrimp and Orzo Salad 24
6. Herb Crusted Whitefish 24
7. Greek Turkey Burgers 24
8. Lentil Spinach Curry 24
9. Tomato Basil Cod 25
10. Chickpea Spinach Stew 25
11. Citrus Marinated Swordfish 25
12. Zucchini Noodle Primavera 26
13. Olive Roasted Chicken 26
14. Quinoa Stuffed Eggplant 26
15. Feta Crusted Salmon 26
16. Spinach Mushroom Frittata 27
17. Greek Yogurt Marinated Chicken 27
18. Mediterranean Tofu Stir Fry 27
19. Baked Cod with Tomatoes 28
20. Lemony Garlic Shrimp 28

SOUPS 29

1. Lentil Veggie Soup 30
2. Tomato Basil Bisque 30
3. Spinach Chickpea Soup 30
4. Greek Lemon Chicken 30
5. Minestrone Delight 31
6. Roasted Red Pepper 31
7. Zucchini Herb Soup 31
8. Seafood Chowder 31
9. Mediterranean Bean Soup 32
10. Quinoa Vegetable Stew 32
11. Cauliflower Curry Soup 32
12. White Bean Rosemary 33
13. Fisherman's Bouillabaisse 33
14. Broccoli Almond Soup 33
15. Eggplant Tomato Bisque 33
16. Chicken Orzo Soup 34
17. Spinach Feta Chowder 34

18. Gazpacho Andaluz   34
19. Artichoke Heart Soup   34
20. Pumpkin Walnut Bisque   35

POULTRY   36

1. Lemon Herb Chicken   37
2. Greek Yogurt Marinade   37
3. Mediterranean Stuffed Turkey   37
4. Balsamic Glazed Quail   37
5. Rosemary Roast Chicken   38
6. Olive Oil Grilled Turkey   38
7. Herbed Chicken Skewers   38
8. Citrus Marinated Duck   38
9. Garlic Roasted Cornish Hens   39
10. Yogurt Mint Chicken   39
11. Tomato Basil Turkey   39
12. Almond Crusted Chicken   40
13. Lemon Thyme Turkey   40
14. Greek Lemon Chicken   40
15. Mediterranean Pesto Chicken   40
16. Feta Stuffed Chicken   41
17. Olive Rosemary Roast Hen   41
18. Herb Grilled Quail   41
19. Orange Glazed Turkey   42
20. Greek Souvlaki Chicken   42

BEEF AND PORK   43

1. Herb Grilled Steak   44
2. Mediterranean Beef Skewers   44
3. Pork Tenderloin Citrus   44
4. Greek Lamb Meatballs   44
5. Balsamic Glazed Pork   45
6. Rosemary Beef Stir-Fry   45
7. Lemon Garlic Pork Chops   45
8. Olive Crusted Beef   46
9. Feta Stuffed Pork   46
10. Yogurt Marinated Lamb   46
11. Spinach Stuffed Beef   46
12. Mediterranean Pork Roast   47
13. Greek Style Burgers   47
14. Herbed Pork Medallions   47
15. Tomato Basil Beef   48
16. Orange Glazed Pork   48
17. Mediterranean Beef Stew   48
18. Greek Pork Souvlaki   48
19. Lemon Thyme Steak   49
20. Olive Braised Pork   49

SIDE DISHES   50

1. Greek Salad   51
2. Lemon Roasted Veggies   51
3. Hummus Trio   51
4. Olive Tapenade   51
5. Quinoa Tabbouleh   52
6. Feta Stuffed Peppers   52
7. Garlic Spinach Saute   52
8. Tomato Cucumber Salad   52
9. Eggplant Caponata   53
10. Mediterranean Rice Pilaf   53
11. Roasted Red Onions   53
12. Greek Yogurt Dip   53
13. Balsamic Grilled Asparagus   54
14. BArtichoke Hearts Saute   54
15. Chickpea Cucumber Salad   54
16. Roasted Brussels Sprouts   54
17. Spinach Feta Stuffed Mushrooms   55
18. Caprese Skewers   55
19. Zucchini Ribbon Salad   55
20. Roasted Garlic Cauliflower   56

VEGETABLES AND GRAINS   57

1. Quinoa Stuffed Peppers   58
2. Greek Chickpea Salad   58
3. Spinach Mushroom Risotto   58
4. Lemon Herb Couscous   58
5. Ratatouille with Polenta   59
6. Zucchini Noodle Stir Fry   59
7. Mediterranean Lentil Soup   59
8. Stuffed Eggplant Boats   60
9. Farro Vegetable Pilaf   60
10. Tomato Basil Bulgur   60
11. Roasted Vegetable Quinoa   60
12. Greek Style Rice   61
13. Caprese Orzo Salad   61
14. Spaghetti Squash Primavera   61
15. Mediterranean Barley Bowl   62
16. Ratatouille Stuffed Bell Peppers   62
17. Herbed Brown Rice   62
18. Eggplant and Farro Casserole   63
19. Cauliflower Fried Rice   63
20. Greek Style Pasta   63

SALADS   65

1. Greek Quinoa Salad   66
2. Mediterranean Chickpea Salad   66
3. Tomato Basil Salad   66
4. Cucumber Feta Salad   66
5. Tuna White Bean Salad   67

6. Greek Salad Wraps 67
7. Minty Watermelon Salad 67
8. Orzo Spinach Salad 67
9. Roasted Beet Salad 68
10. Caprese Salad Skewers 68
11. Lemon Herb Couscous Salad 68
12. Arugula Pomegranate Salad 68
13. Zesty Shrimp Salad 69
14. Avocado Tomato Salad 69
15. Spinach Berry Salad 69
16. Grilled Eggplant Salad 70
17. Kale Quinoa Salad 70
18. Roasted Red Pepper Salad 70
19. Artichoke Heart Salad 70
20. Mango Avocado Salad 71

SNACKS AND APPETIZERS 72

1. Olive Tapenade Crostini 73
2. Greek Yogurt Dip 73
3. Hummus Stuffed Peppers 73
4. Cucumber Feta Bites 73
5. Spinach Artichoke Dip 74
6. Tomato Basil Bruschetta 74
7. Mediterranean Tuna Salad 74
8. Roasted Red Pepper Hummus 74
9. Stuffed Grape Leaves 75
10. Feta Cucumber Boats 75
11. Smoked Salmon Rolls 75
12. Greek Stuffed Mushrooms 75
13. Spiced Almonds Mix 76
14. Zucchini Fritters 76
15. Eggplant Caponata 76
16. Herbed Quinoa Bites 77
17. Lemon Garlic Shrimp Skewers 77
18. Yogurt Cucumber Cups 77
19. Olive Focaccia Slices 77
20. Marinated Olives Platter 78

DESSERTS 79

1. Fruity Yogurt Parfait 80
2. Almond Orange Biscotti 80
3. Greek Yogurt Popsicles 80
4. Berry Chia Pudding 80
5. Roasted Fig Delight 81
6. Dark Chocolate Dipped Strawberries 81
7. Honeyed Almond Bites 81
8. Lemon Ricotta Tartlets 81
9. Pistachio Date Balls 82
10. Baked Apple Slices 82
11. Coconut Rice Pudding 82
12. Watermelon Mint Sorbet 82
13. Greek Yogurt Mousse 83
14. Orange Olive Oil Cake 83
15. Mixed Berry Crumble 83
16. Apricot Walnut Bars 84
17. Chocolate Avocado Mousse 84
18. Walnut Stuffed Dates 84
19. Pomegranate Frozen Yogurt 84
20. Cinnamon Baked Pears 85

MEAL PLAN 86

CONVERSION TABLES 89

BONUS 90

Introduction

What is the Mediterranean Diet?

The Mediterranean diet is a traditional dietary pattern inspired by the eating habits of people living in Mediterranean regions, such as Italy, Greece, Spain and other surrounding countries. This diet is based on a balanced consumption of fresh, nutritious, whole foods and is associated with numerous health benefits.

The main characteristics of the Mediterranean diet include:

Fresh and unprocessed foods: The diet emphasizes the intake of fresh and minimally processed foods, such as fruits, vegetables, legumes, nuts, whole grains, and fish.

Healthy fats: The predominant use of extra virgin olive oil is a mainstay of this diet. Olive oil is rich in monounsaturated fats and antioxidants beneficial for heart health.

Moderate consumption of meat and dairy products: Meat is consumed in moderate amounts, often as part of meals rather than as a main component. Dairy products, such as cheese and yogurt, are consumed in moderate amounts.

High proportion of vegetables and fruits: These foods provide essential vitamins, minerals and fiber. Consumption of a variety of colors and types of vegetables and fruits is encouraged.

Fish and lean protein: Fish is an important source of protein and omega-3 fatty acids, which are beneficial for cardiovascular health. Lean proteins from sources such as legumes, nuts and seeds are preferred over red meat.

Moderate wine consumption: In some versions of the Mediterranean diet, red wine is consumed in moderation with meals. This is associated with beneficial substances such as polyphenols.

Herbs and spices: Herbs and spices are widely used to flavor dishes, reducing the need for added salt.

Regular physical activity and active lifestyle: In addition to diet, a Mediterranean lifestyle includes regular physical activity and reduced stress.

The Mediterranean diet has been associated with several health benefits, including a reduced incidence of heart disease, type 2 diabetes, and some aging-related diseases. However, it is important to note that the Mediterranean diet is not just about specific foods, but also about mindsets and eating habits that promote overall well-being.

A New Way of Life

The Mediterranean diet is not just a simple set of dietary rules; it is conceived as a complete lifestyle that embraces not only what you put on your plate, but also how you relate to food, your body, and your surroundings. This new lifestyle focuses on key principles that go beyond food and extend to your mental health, your physical activity, and your relationship with nature.

This is how the Mediterranean diet can be considered a new way of life:

Mindful Eating: The Mediterranean diet promotes paying attention to the food you eat. Instead of absent-minded or hurried eating, the Mediterranean approach encourages you to enjoy the flavors, recognize satiety, and practice gratitude for what you eat.

Regular Physical Activity: The Mediterranean diet is not only about what you eat, but also how you move. Regular physical activity is an integral part of the Mediterranean lifestyle. Walking, swimming, dancing and other activities are encouraged to promote heart and overall health.

Socializing and Sharing: Mediterranean communities often share meals with family or friends. This practice promotes a sense of connection and community, reducing solitary, hurried eating.

Relationship with Nature: Many people who follow the Mediterranean diet have access to fresh, often local and seasonal ingredients. This connection to locally grown foods and surrounding nature is an important aspect of the Mediterranean lifestyle.

Stress Management: The Mediterranean diet emphasizes stress management through food and other relaxing activities, such as socializing and movement. This contributes to mental and physical balance.

Balance: The Mediterranean diet is not based on extreme restrictions or drastic diets. Rather, it is a balance between different food groups, including fruits, vegetables, proteins, whole grains, and healthy fats.

Mental Health: The focus on an abundance of fresh, colorful and nutritious foods can have a positive impact on mental health, helping to reduce the risk of depression and anxiety.

Sustainability: The Mediterranean diet is often associated with sustainable choices, such as eating local and seasonal produce, which helps reduce environmental impact.

In summary, the Mediterranean diet as a new lifestyle is not just about the food you put on your plate, but encourages a holistic approach to health and well-being. It represents a way of life that can promote a better quality of life, both physically and mentally.

Expectation

From the Mediterranean diet, you can expect a number of health and wellness benefits, both short- and long-term. However, it is important to keep in mind that results may vary from person to person depending on individual habits, current health status and other factors. Here is what you can generally expect from the Mediterranean diet:

Improved Cardiovascular Health: The Mediterranean diet has been associated with reduced risk of heart disease. High consumption of healthy fats such as olive oil and omega-3 fatty acids found in fish can help reduce bad cholesterol (LDL) and improve artery health.

Weight Control: The Mediterranean diet emphasizes eating whole foods, which are rich in fiber and nutrients that can promote a longer lasting sense of satiety. This can help control appetite and manage body weight.

Diabetes Management: Because of its emphasis on low-glycemic index and fiber-rich foods, the Mediterranean diet can help stabilize blood sugar levels, providing support in managing type 2 diabetes.

Improved Brain Function: The omega-3 fatty acids found in fish, along with antioxidants found in fruits and vegetables, can help maintain brain health and reduce the risk of cognitive decline.

Digestive Health: High fiber consumption from whole grains, vegetables, and legumes can promote a healthy digestive tract and regular bowel function.

Inflammation Reduction: Foods found in the Mediterranean diet, such as healthy oils, vegetables and spices, can help reduce inflammation in the body, which is linked to many chronic diseases.

Skin Health: Antioxidants found in fruits, vegetables and olive oil can help maintain healthy, glowing skin.

Increased Energy: The balanced approach of the Mediterranean diet, which includes a variety of nutritious foods, can help keep energy levels steady throughout the day.

Mood Enhancement: Intake of foods rich in nutrients and antioxidants can positively influence mood and help reduce the risk of depression.

Promotion of Longevity: Mediterranean populations are often associated with superior longevity. Although multiple factors contribute to this outcome, a balanced, nutrient-rich Mediterranean diet certainly plays a role.

Remember that the Mediterranean diet is a long-term approach and its benefits may not be immediately apparent. It is important to adopt it as a lifestyle and not just as a temporary diet to achieve the best results. If you have pre-existing health conditions or special dietary needs, always consult a health professional before making significant changes to your diet.

The Food Pyramid

The food pyramid of the Mediterranean diet is a visual representation of the typical dietary approach of Mediterranean populations. It offers guidance on how to structure meals and food choices in a way that follows the basic principles of the Mediterranean diet. The pyramid emphasizes the importance of various foods and highlights those that should be eaten more frequently and in larger quantities.

Here is a description of the various levels of the Mediterranean diet food pyramid, starting from the base:

Physical activity and active living: The base of the pyramid emphasizes the importance of regular physical activity and an active lifestyle. Exercise is an essential component of the Mediterranean lifestyle.

Hydration: This level includes water as the main beverage. Water is essential for hydration and proper functioning of the body.

Fruits, vegetables, legumes and nuts: This layer represents the largest part of the pyramid, indicating that you should consume a wide variety of fruits, vegetables, legumes and nuts. These foods provide essential fiber, vitamins, minerals and antioxidants.

Whole grains and grain products: This level includes foods such as whole grain breads, whole grains, brown rice, and whole grain pasta. Whole grains are a lasting source of energy and would provide important nutrients.

Olive oil: Olive oil is a major source of healthy fats in the Mediterranean diet. It is used for cooking and seasoning, providing monounsaturated fats and beneficial antioxidants.

Dairy (or alternatives) and fish: This level represents the moderate intake of dairy products, preferably fresh cheese and yogurt. Fish is another important source of protein, omega-3 fatty acids and essential nutrients.

Lean meat and poultry: This level includes lean meat and poultry consumed in moderate amounts. Howe-

-ver, in the traditional Mediterranean diet, meat consumption is lower than other protein sources.

Occasional consumption: At the top of the pyramid, we find foods such as cakes, sweets and processed meats. These foods should be consumed only occasionally and in limited quantities.

The Mediterranean diet food pyramid emphasizes the importance of a plant-based diet, rich in fruits, vegetables, whole grains, legumes and healthy fats such as olive oil. The pyramid also emphasizes balance and moderation, encouraging moderate consumption of animal protein and sweets. Remember that the pyramid is a general guide and can be adapted to your individual dietary preferences and needs.

20 FAQ

1. What exactly is the Mediterranean diet?
The Mediterranean diet is an eating pattern inspired by the culinary habits of people living in the Mediterranean regions. It is based on abundant consumption of fruits, vegetables, whole grains, legumes, fish, healthy fats such as olive oil, and moderate consumption of lean meat and dairy products.

2. What are the basic principles of the Mediterranean diet?
The basic principles of the Mediterranean diet include abundant intake of plant-based foods, consumption of healthy fats such as olive oil, regular consumption of fish, limited consumption of red meat, moderate consumption of red wine (if desired), and an emphasis on physical activity and socializing.

3. What foods are typical of the Mediterranean diet?
Typical foods include fruits, vegetables, legumes, whole grains, fish, olive oil, nuts, seeds, herbs, spices, low-fat dairy products, yogurt, cheese, eggs, and moderate consumption of lean meat.

4. What are the health benefits associated with the Mediterranean diet?
The Mediterranean diet is associated with benefits such as reduced risk of heart disease, weight control, diabetes management, brain health, improved mood, skin health, and potentially increased longevity.

5. Can I lose weight by following the Mediterranean diet?
Yes, many people lose weight by following the Mediterranean diet because of its emphasis on foods that are nutritious, high in fiber, and low in saturated fat.

6. What is the role of olive oil in the Mediterranean diet?
Olive oil is a major source of healthy fats, particularly monounsaturated fatty acids. It is used as a primary fat source in the Mediterranean diet, with cardiovascular health and antioxidant benefits.

5

7. What can I drink in the Mediterranean diet?

In addition to water, you can drink tea, coffee, herbal infusions and, if you wish, moderate consumption of red wine with meals.

8. Can I follow the Mediterranean diet if I am a vegetarian or vegan?

Absolutely. The Mediterranean diet can be adapted to vegetarian or vegan preferences by replacing animal protein sources with legumes, nuts, seeds, tofu and other plant-based alternatives.

9. What are the best types of fish to consume in the Mediterranean diet?

Fatty fish rich in omega-3 fatty acids, such as salmon, tuna, sardines, and anchovies, are particularly beneficial in the Mediterranean diet.

10. What is the relationship between the Mediterranean diet and heart disease prevention?

The Mediterranean diet has been linked to reduced risk of heart disease due to its content of healthy fats, antioxidants, and nutrients that promote heart health.

11. Can I consume red meat in the Mediterranean diet?

Yes, red meat is consumed in limited amounts in the Mediterranean diet. It is preferable to choose lean cuts and consume it occasionally.

12. How many fruits and vegetables should I consume per day?

The goal is to consume at least 5 servings of fruits and vegetables per day, providing a variety of colors and nutrients.

13. How can I adapt the Mediterranean diet to my personal tastes?

You can customize the Mediterranean diet by choosing foods you like within the recommended food groups and experimenting with herbs, spices and cooking methods.

14. What makes the Mediterranean diet different from other popular diets?

The Mediterranean diet focuses on balance and variety, promoting the consumption of fresh, whole foods rather than extreme restrictions.

15. Does the Mediterranean diet include snacks?

Yes, you can include healthy snacks such as fruits, nuts and cut vegetables in the Mediterranean diet.

16. What foods should I limit or avoid in the Mediterranean diet?

You should limit your consumption of foods high in added sugars, saturated fats, and highly processed foods.

17. Can I eat bread in the Mediterranean diet?

Yes, whole grain bread is part of the Mediterranean diet. It is preferable to choose whole grain bread instead of refined bread.

18. What is the Mediterranean approach to alcohol?

If you wish, you can consume red wine in moderation during meals. However, it is important to stay within the recommended limits for alcohol consumption.

19. Do I have to follow the Mediterranean diet strictly or can I make exceptions?

Flexibility is allowed. You can make occasional exceptions, but still try to maintain overall balance and healthy choices.

20. How can I start following the Mediterranean diet?

Start by adding more fruits, vegetables, whole grains and healthy fats to your diet. Reduce your consumption of highly processed foods and take small steps toward a more Mediterranean lifestyle.

Remember that these answers are general guidelines and may vary according to individual needs. If you have specific questions, it is always best to consult a health professional or dietitian.

Breakfast

1. Berry Parfait Delight

Preparation time: 10 minutes
Servings: 2

Ingredients:

- 1 cup Greek yogurt
- 1 cup mixed berries (strawberries, blueberries, raspberries)
- 2 tablespoons honey
- 2 tablespoons granola
- 1 tablespoon chopped almonds
- Fresh mint leaves (for garnish)

Instructions:

1. In two serving glasses, layer Greek yogurt.
2. Add a layer of mixed berries on top.
3. Drizzle honey over the berries.
4. Sprinkle granola and chopped almonds on the honey.
5. Repeat the layers.
6. Garnish with fresh mint leaves.
7. Serve immediately and enjoy!

Nutritional Information (per serving):
Cal: 230 | Carbs: 32g | Pro: 12g | Fat: 6g | Sugars: 25g | Fiber: 4g | Sodium: 50mg

2. Greek Yogurt Bowl

Preparation time: 5 minutes
Servings: 2

Ingredients:

- 2 cups Greek yogurt
- 1 medium banana, sliced
- 1/2 cup mixed nuts (almonds, walnuts, pistachios)
- 2 tablespoons honey
- 1/2 teaspoon cinnamon
- 1 tablespoon chia seeds

Instructions:

1. Divide Greek yogurt into two bowls.
2. Top with banana slices and mixed nuts.
3. Drizzle honey over the yogurt.
4. Sprinkle cinnamon and chia seeds.
5. Mix well and enjoy!

Nutritional Information (per serving):
Cal: 320 | Carbs: 30g | Pro: 15g | Fat: 18g | Sugars: 15g | Fiber: 7g | Sodium: 50mg

3. Avocado Toast Feast

Preparation time: 10 minutes

Servings: 2

Ingredients:

- 2 slices whole grain bread
- 1 avocado, sliced
- 1 small tomato, sliced
- 2 boiled eggs, sliced
- Salt and pepper to taste
- Red pepper flakes (optional)
- Fresh basil leaves (for garnish)

Instructions:

1. Toast the whole grain bread slices.
2. Top each slice with avocado slices.
3. Arrange tomato and boiled egg slices over the avocado.
4. Season with salt, pepper, and red pepper flakes.
5. Garnish with fresh basil leaves.
6. Serve immediately and enjoy!

Nutritional Information (per serving):
Cal: 280 | Carbs: 22g | Pro: 15g | Fat: 16g | Sugars: 2g | Fiber: 10g | Sodium: 220mg

4. Spinach Omelet Roll

Preparation time: 15 minutes
Servings: 2

Ingredients:

- 4 large eggs
- 1/4 cup milk
- Salt and pepper to taste
- 1 cup fresh spinach leaves
- 1/2 cup feta cheese, crumbled
- 1/4 cup diced tomatoes

Instructions:

1. In a bowl, whisk eggs, milk, salt, and pepper.
2. Heat a non-stick skillet over medium heat.
3. Pour half of the egg mixture into the skillet, spreading evenly.
4. Cook until the edges set, then add spinach, feta, and tomatoes.
5. Gently fold the omelet in half and cook until eggs are fully set.
6. Carefully roll the omelet onto a plate.
7. Repeat for the second omelet.
8. Slice each roll in half and serve.

Nutritional Information (per serving):
Cal: 230 | Carbs: 3g | Pro: 18g | Fat: 16g | Sugars: 1g | Fiber: 1g | Sodium: 420mg

5. Almond Chia Pudding

Preparation time: 5 minutes (+ chilling time)
Servings: 2

Ingredients:

- 1 cup unsweetened almond milk
- 1/4 cup chia seeds
- 1 tablespoon honey
- 1/4 teaspoon vanilla extract
- 2 tablespoons slivered almonds
- Fresh berries (for topping)

Instructions:

1. In a bowl, mix almond milk, chia seeds, honey, and vanilla.
2. Stir well and refrigerate for at least 2 hours, or overnight.
3. Before serving, stir the pudding and divide into two bowls.
4. Top with slivered almonds and fresh berries.
5. Enjoy the creamy chia pudding!

Nutritional Information (per serving):
Cal: 180 | Carbs: 14g | Pro: 5g | Fat: 12g | Sugars: 6g | Fiber: 10g | Sodium: 75mg

6. Mediterranean Frittata

Preparation time: 20 minutes
Servings: 2

Ingredients:

- 4 large eggs
- 1/4 cup milk
- Salt and pepper to taste
- 1/2 cup cherry tomatoes, halved
- 1/4 cup chopped spinach
- 1/4 cup crumbled feta cheese
- 2 tablespoons chopped fresh herbs (e.g., basil, parsley)

Instructions:

1. Preheat the oven to 350°F (175°C).
2. In a bowl, whisk eggs, milk, salt, and pepper.
3. Heat an oven-safe skillet over medium heat.
4. Pour the egg mixture into the skillet.
5. Add cherry tomatoes, spinach, and feta cheese evenly.
6. Cook for a few minutes until the edges set.
7. Transfer the skillet to the oven and bake for about 10 minutes.
8. Sprinkle fresh herbs over the frittata.
9. Slice and serve the frittata directly from the skillet.

Nutritional Information (per serving):
Cal: 220 | Carbs: 6g | Pro: 16g | Fat: 15g | Sugars: 3g | Fiber: 1g | Sodium: 380mg

7. Whole Grain Pancakes

Preparation time: 15 minutes
Servings: 2

Ingredients:

- 1 cup whole wheat flour
- 1 tablespoon honey
- 1 teaspoon baking powder
- 1/2 teaspoon cinnamon
- 1 cup unsweetened almond milk
- 1 large egg
- Fresh berries (for topping)

Instructions:

1. In a bowl, whisk flour, honey, baking powder, and cinnamon.
2. In another bowl, mix almond milk and egg.
3. Combine wet and dry ingredients, mixing until just combined.
4. Heat a non-stick skillet over medium heat.
5. Pour 1/4 cup of batter for each pancake.
6. Cook until bubbles form on the surface, then flip and cook the other side.
7. Stack pancakes and top with fresh berries.
8. Enjoy fluffy whole grain pancakes!

Nutritional Information (per serving):
Cal: 270 | Carbs: 49g | Pro: 9g | Fat: 4g | Sugars: 12g | Fiber: 8g | Sodium: 310mg

8. Veggie Breakfast Wrap

Preparation time: 10 minutes
Servings: 2

Ingredients:

- 2 whole wheat tortillas
- 4 large eggs, scrambled
- 1/2 cup baby spinach leaves
- 1/2 cup diced bell peppers
- 1/4 cup diced red onion
- 1/4 cup crumbled goat cheese

Instructions:

1. Warm the tortillas according to package instructions.
2. Divide scrambled eggs between tortillas.
3. Layer spinach, bell peppers, and red onion.
4. Sprinkle crumbled goat cheese on top.
5. Fold in the sides of the tortilla and roll.
6. Serve the breakfast wraps warm.

Nutritional Information (per serving):
Cal: 320 | Carbs: 23g | Pro: 20g | Fat: 17g | Sugars:
5g | Fiber: 5g | Sodium: 480mg

9. Smoked Salmon Plate

Preparation time: 10 minutes
Servings: 2

Ingredients:

- 4 slices whole grain bread
- 4 ounces smoked salmon
- 1/4 cup Greek yogurt
- 1 tablespoon capers
- 1/4 cup thinly sliced red onion
- Fresh dill (for garnish)

Instructions:

1. Toast the whole grain bread slices.
2. Spread Greek yogurt over the toast.
3. Top with smoked salmon slices.
4. Sprinkle capers and red onion.
5. Garnish with fresh dill.
6. Serve the salmon plate open-faced.

Nutritional Information (per serving):
Cal: 250 | Carbs: 20g | Pro: 18g | Fat: 10g | Sugars:
3g | Fiber: 3g | Sodium: 760mg

10. Quinoa Breakfast Bowl

Preparation time: 15 minutes
Servings: 2

Ingredients:

- 1 cup cooked quinoa
- 1/2 cup plain Greek yogurt
- 1/4 cup mixed berries
- 2 tablespoons chopped nuts (e.g., almonds, walnuts)
- 1 tablespoon honey
- 1/2 teaspoon vanilla extract
- Pinch of cinnamon

Instructions:

1. In a bowl, mix cooked quinoa and Greek yogurt.
2. Top with mixed berries and chopped nuts.
3. Drizzle honey and vanilla extract.
4. Sprinkle a pinch of cinnamon.
5. Mix well and enjoy the quinoa bowl!

Nutritional Information (per serving):
Cal: 280 | Carbs: 34g | Pro: 14g | Fat: 9g | Sugars:
15g | Fiber: 4g | Sodium: 60mg

11. Tomato Basil Scramble

Preparation time: 15 minutes
Servings: 2

Ingredients:

- 4 large eggs
- 1 medium tomato, diced
- 1/4 cup chopped fresh basil
- 2 tablespoons grated Parmesan cheese
- Salt and pepper to taste
- 1 tablespoon olive oil
- Whole grain toast (for serving)

Instructions:

1. In a bowl, whisk eggs, diced tomato, chopped basil, and Parmesan cheese.
2. Heat olive oil in a non-stick skillet over medium heat.
3. Pour the egg mixture into the skillet.
4. Cook and gently scramble the eggs until they are fully set.
5. Season with salt and pepper.
6. Serve the scramble with whole grain toast.

Nutritional Information (per serving):
Cal: 210 | Carbs: 4g | Pro: 14g | Fat: 15g | Sugars:
2g | Fiber: 1g | Sodium: 230mg

12. Cottage Cheese Delight

Preparation time: 10 minutes
Servings: 2

Ingredients:

- 1 cup low-fat cottage cheese
- 1/2 cup mixed berries
- 2 tablespoons chopped walnuts
- 1 tablespoon honey
- 1/2 teaspoon vanilla extract
- Fresh mint leaves (for garnish)

Instructions:

1. Divide cottage cheese between two bowls.
2. Top with mixed berries and chopped walnuts.
3. Drizzle honey and vanilla extract.
4. Garnish with fresh mint leaves.
5. Enjoy the cottage cheese delight!

Nutritional Information (per serving):
Cal: 220 | Carbs: 15g | Pro: 18g | Fat: 10g | Sugars:
10g | Fiber: 2g | Sodium: 480mg

13. Olive Tapenade Toast

Preparation time: 10 minutes
Servings: 2

Ingredients:

- 4 slices whole grain bread
- 1/4 cup olive tapenade
- 2 ounces sliced mozzarella cheese
- 1/4 cup arugula leaves
- 1 tablespoon balsamic vinegar
- Salt and pepper to taste

Instructions:

1. Toast the whole grain bread slices.
2. Spread olive tapenade over the toast.
3. Top with sliced mozzarella and arugula.
4. Drizzle balsamic vinegar over the toppings.
5. Season with salt and pepper.
6. Serve the tapenade toast open-faced.

Nutritional Information (per serving):
Cal: 250 | Carbs: 24g | Pro: 9g | Fat: 14g | Sugars: 3g | Fiber: 5g | Sodium: 550mg

14. Mixed Berry Smoothie

Preparation time: 5 minutes
Servings: 2

Ingredients:

- 1 cup mixed berries (strawberries, blueberries, raspberries)
- 1 ripe banana
- 1 cup unsweetened almond milk
- 1/2 cup plain Greek yogurt
- 1 tablespoon chia seeds
- 1 tablespoon honey (optional)
- Ice cubes

Instructions:

1. Blend mixed berries, banana, almond milk, and Greek yogurt until smooth.
2. Add chia seeds and honey (if using) and blend again.
3. Add ice cubes and blend to desired consistency.
4. Pour into glasses and serve the mixed berry smoothie.

Nutritional Information (per serving):
Cal: 180 | Carbs: 31g | Pro: 7g | Fat: 4g | Sugars: 18g | Fiber: 7g | Sodium: 110mg

15. Egg and Spinach Muffins

Preparation time: 20 minutes
Servings: 2 (6 muffins total)

Ingredients:

- 4 large eggs
- 1/4 cup milk
- Salt and pepper to taste
- 1 cup chopped spinach
- 1/4 cup diced bell peppers
- 1/4 cup diced red onion

Instructions:

1. Preheat the oven to 350°F (175°C) and grease a muffin tin.
2. In a bowl, whisk eggs, milk, salt, and pepper.
3. Stir in chopped spinach, bell peppers, and red onion.
4. Pour the egg mixture evenly into the muffin tin.
5. Bake for about 15-18 minutes until the muffins are set.
6. Allow them to cool slightly before serving.

Nutritional Information (per serving):
Cal: 150 | Carbs: 7g | Pro: 12g | Fat: 8g | Sugars: 4g | Fiber: 2g | Sodium: 290mg

16. Oatmeal Banana Bowl

Preparation time: 10 minutes
Servings: 2

Ingredients:

- 1 cup rolled oats
- 2 cups water or unsweetened almond milk
- 1 ripe banana, mashed
- 1/4 cup chopped nuts (e.g., almonds, walnuts)
- 1/2 teaspoon cinnamon
- 1 tablespoon honey
- Fresh berries (for topping)

Instructions:

1. In a saucepan, bring water or almond milk to a boil.
2. Stir in rolled oats and reduce heat to low.
3. Cook for about 5 minutes, stirring occasionally.
4. Remove from heat and stir in mashed banana, nuts, and cinnamon.
5. Drizzle honey over the oatmeal.
6. Top with fresh berries and serve.

Nutritional Information (per serving):
Cal: 280 | Carbs: 42g | Pro: 7g | Fat: 10g | Sugars: 13g | Fiber: 6g | Sodium: 10mg

17. Tofu Scramble Plate

Preparation time: 15 minutes
Servings: 2

Ingredients:

- 8 ounces firm tofu, crumbled
- 1/2 cup diced bell peppers
- 1/4 cup diced red onion
- 1/2 teaspoon turmeric
- Salt and pepper to taste
- 1 tablespoon olive oil
- Fresh parsley (for garnish)

Instructions:

1. Heat olive oil in a skillet over medium heat.
2. Add diced bell peppers and red onion. Sauté until softened.
3. Add crumbled tofu and turmeric. Cook for a few minutes.
4. Season with salt and pepper.
5. Garnish with fresh parsley.
6. Serve the tofu scramble with whole grain toast.

Nutritional Information (per serving):
Cal: 180 | Carbs: 10g | Pro: 12g | Fat: 11g | Sugars: 4g | Fiber: 3g | Sodium: 240mg

18. Mediterranean Shakshuka

Preparation time: 25 minutes
Servings: 2

Ingredients:

- 1 tablespoon olive oil
- 1/2 cup diced onion
- 1/2 cup diced bell peppers
- 1 clove garlic, minced
- 1 can (14 oz) diced tomatoes
- 1/2 teaspoon ground cumin
- 1/2 teaspoon paprika
- Salt and pepper to taste
- 4 large eggs
- Fresh parsley (for garnish)

Instructions:

1. Heat olive oil in a skillet over medium heat.
2. Sauté diced onion and bell peppers until softened.
3. Add minced garlic and cook for 1 minute.
4. Stir in diced tomatoes, cumin, paprika, salt, and pepper.
5. Create wells in the mixture and crack eggs into them.
6. Cover and cook until eggs are set to your liking.
7. Garnish with fresh parsley.

8. Serve shakshuka with whole grain bread.

Nutritional Information (per serving):
Cal: 210 | Carbs: 14g | Pro: 12g | Fat: 13g | Sugars: 8g | Fiber: 4g | Sodium: 500mg

19. Almond Butter Waffles

Preparation time: 20 minutes
Servings: 2 (4 waffles total)

Ingredients:

- 1 cup whole wheat flour
- 1 tablespoon honey
- 1 teaspoon baking powder
- 1/4 teaspoon cinnamon
- 1 cup unsweetened almond milk
- 1/4 cup almond butter
- 1 large egg

Instructions:

1. Preheat and lightly grease a waffle iron.
2. In a bowl, whisk flour, honey, baking powder, and cinnamon.
3. In another bowl, mix almond milk, almond butter, and egg.
4. Combine wet and dry ingredients until just combined.
5. Pour batter onto the waffle iron and cook according to instructions.
6. Repeat for the remaining batter.
7. Serve almond butter waffles with fresh fruit.

Nutritional Information (per serving):
Cal: 350 | Carbs: 39g | Pro: 12g | Fat: 18g | Sugars: 8g | Fiber: 7g | Sodium: 430mg

20. Walnut Raisin Porridge

Preparation time: 15 minutes
Servings: 2

Ingredients:

- 1 cup old-fashioned oats
- 2 cups water or unsweetened almond milk
- 1/4 cup chopped walnuts
- 1/4 cup raisins
- 1/2 teaspoon cinnamon
- 1 tablespoon maple syrup
- Splash of vanilla extract

Instructions:

1. In a saucepan, bring water or almond milk to a boil.
2. Stir in oats and reduce heat to low.

3. Cook for about 5-7 minutes, stirring occasionally.
4. Stir in chopped walnuts and raisins.
5. Add cinnamon, maple syrup, and vanilla extract.
6. Continue cooking until desired consistency is reached.
7. Serve the walnut raisin porridge warm.

Nutritional Information (per serving):
Cal: 280 | Carbs: 46g | Pro: 7g | Fat: 8g | Sugars: 16g | Fiber: 6g | Sodium: 10mg

First Dishes

1. Mediterranean Zucchini Pasta

Preparation time: 15 minutes
Servings: 2

Ingredients:

- 6 oz whole wheat spaghetti
- 1 medium zucchini, spiralized
- 1 cup cherry tomatoes, halved
- 2 cloves garlic, minced
- 2 tablespoons extra virgin olive oil
- 1/4 cup crumbled feta cheese
- Salt and pepper to taste

Instructions:

1. Cook whole wheat spaghetti according to package instructions. Drain and set aside.
2. In a large skillet, heat olive oil over medium heat.
3. Add minced garlic and sauté for about 1 minute, until fragrant.
4. Add spiralized zucchini and halved cherry tomatoes. Sauté for about 2-3 minutes, until slightly softened.
5. Toss cooked spaghetti into the skillet and mix well.
6. Season with salt and pepper to taste.
7. Divide the pasta between two plates.
8. Sprinkle crumbled feta cheese over the pasta.
9. Serve the Mediterranean zucchini pasta as a light and flavorful dish.

Nutritional Information (per serving):
Cal: 380 | Carbs: 54g | Pro: 13g | Fat: 14g | Sugars: 7g | Fiber: 9g | Sodium: 350mg

2. Tomato Basil Linguine

Preparation time: 10 minutes
Servings: 2

Ingredients:

- 6 oz whole wheat linguine
- 1 cup diced tomatoes
- 1/4 cup chopped fresh basil
- 2 cloves garlic, minced
- 2 tablespoons extra virgin olive oil
- 1/4 teaspoon red pepper flakes (optional)
- Salt and pepper to taste

Instructions:

1. Cook whole wheat linguine according to package instructions. Drain and set aside.
2. In a skillet, heat olive oil over medium heat.
3. Add minced garlic and red pepper flakes. Sauté for about 1 minute.
4. Add diced tomatoes and cook for another 2-3 minutes.

5. Toss cooked linguine into the skillet.
6. Stir in chopped fresh basil.
7. Season with salt and pepper to taste.
8. Divide the pasta between two plates.
9. Serve the tomato basil linguine as a simple and satisfying dish.

Nutritional Information (per serving):
Cal: 330 | Carbs: 52g | Pro: 10g | Fat: 10g | Sugars: 4g | Fiber: 8g | Sodium: 220mg

3. Garlic Spinach Spaghetti

Preparation time: 15 minutes
Servings: 2

Ingredients:

- 6 oz whole wheat spaghetti
- 4 cups baby spinach
- 4 cloves garlic, minced
- 2 tablespoons extra virgin olive oil
- 1/4 teaspoon red pepper flakes
- Salt and pepper to taste

Instructions:

1. Cook whole wheat spaghetti according to package instructions. Drain and set aside.
2. In a large skillet, heat olive oil over medium heat.
3. Add minced garlic and red pepper flakes. Sauté for about 1 minute, until fragrant.
4. Add baby spinach to the skillet and sauté until wilted.
5. Toss cooked spaghetti into the skillet and mix well.
6. Season with salt and pepper to taste.
7. Divide the pasta between two plates.
8. Serve the garlic spinach spaghetti as a quick and nutritious dish.

Nutritional Information (per serving):
Cal: 320 | Carbs: 54g | Pro: 9g | Fat: 9g | Sugars: 3g | Fiber: 9g | Sodium: 240mg

4. Lemon Herb Orzo Soup

Preparation time: 15 minutes
Cook time: 25 minutes
Servings: 2

Ingredients:

- 1/2 cup whole wheat orzo pasta
- 4 cups low-sodium vegetable broth
- 1 cup diced carrots
- 1 cup chopped kale or spinach
- Juice and zest of 1 lemon
- 2 tablespoons chopped fresh dill or parsley
- Salt and pepper to taste

Instructions:

1. In a pot, bring low-sodium vegetable broth to a boil.
2. Stir in whole wheat orzo pasta and diced carrots. Cook for about 10-12 minutes, until the pasta is tender.
3. Add chopped kale or spinach and cook for another 3-4 minutes, until wilted.
4. Stir in lemon juice and zest, and chopped fresh dill or parsley.
5. Season with salt and pepper to taste.
6. Divide the soup between two bowls.
7. Serve the lemon herb orzo soup as a comforting and nourishing dish.

Nutritional Information (per serving):
Cal: 240 | Carbs: 48g | Pro: 6g | Fat: 1g | Sugars: 5g | Fiber: 6g | Sodium: 440mg

5. Chickpea Pasta Primavera

Preparation time: 15 minutes
Cook time: 15 minutes
Servings: 2

Ingredients:

- 6 oz chickpea pasta
- 1 cup mixed vegetables (bell peppers, zucchini, cherry tomatoes), diced
- 2 cloves garlic, minced
- 2 tablespoons extra virgin olive oil
- 1/4 cup grated Parmesan cheese
- Salt and pepper to taste

Instructions:

1. Cook chickpea pasta according to package instructions. Drain and set aside.
2. In a large skillet, heat olive oil over medium heat.
3. Add minced garlic and sauté for about 1 minute, until fragrant.
4. Add mixed vegetables to the skillet and sauté for about 4-5 minutes, until slightly softened.
5. Toss cooked chickpea pasta into the skillet and mix well.
6. Season with salt and pepper to taste.
7. Divide the pasta between two plates.
8. Sprinkle grated Parmesan cheese over the pasta.
9. Serve the chickpea pasta primavera as a protein-rich and flavorful dish.

Nutritional Information (per serving):
Cal: 370 | Carbs: 46g | Pro: 15g | Fat: 15g | Sugars: 5g | Fiber: 9g | Sodium: 330mg

6. Greek Feta Penne

Preparation time: 10 minutes

Cook time: 15 minutes
Servings: 2

Ingredients:

- 6 oz whole wheat penne pasta
- 1 cup diced cucumbers
- 1/2 cup diced tomatoes
- 1/4 cup crumbled feta cheese
- 2 tablespoons chopped fresh dill
- 2 tablespoons extra virgin olive oil
- Salt and pepper to taste

Instructions:

1. Cook whole wheat penne pasta according to package instructions. Drain and set aside.
2. In a bowl, combine cooked penne pasta, diced cucumbers, diced tomatoes, crumbled feta cheese, chopped fresh dill, and extra virgin olive oil.
3. Season with salt and pepper to taste.
4. Divide the pasta between two plates.
5. Serve the Greek feta penne as a refreshing and vibrant dish.

Nutritional Information (per serving):
Cal: 360 | Carbs: 49g | Pro: 10g | Fat: 14g | Sugars: 4g | Fiber: 8g | Sodium: 300mg

7. Cauliflower Alfredo Fettuccine

Preparation time: 15 minutes
Cook time: 20 minutes
Servings: 2

Ingredients:

- 6 oz whole wheat fettuccine
- 2 cups cauliflower florets
- 2 cloves garlic, minced
- 1/2 cup low-sodium vegetable broth
- 1/4 cup grated Parmesan cheese
- 2 tablespoons extra virgin olive oil
- Salt and pepper to taste

Instructions:

1. Cook whole wheat fettuccine according to package instructions. Drain and set aside.
2. Steam cauliflower florets until tender.
3. In a blender, combine steamed cauliflower, minced garlic, low-sodium vegetable broth, grated Parmesan cheese, and extra virgin olive oil. Blend until smooth and creamy.
4. Toss cooked fettuccine with the cauliflower alfredo sauce.
5. Season with salt and pepper to taste.
6. Divide the pasta between two plates.
7. Serve the cauliflower alfredo fettuccine as a lighter take on a classic favorite.

Nutritional Information (per serving):
Cal: 330 | Carbs: 53g | Pro: 12g | Fat: 10g | Sugars: 3g | Fiber: 10g | Sodium: 280mg

8. Mushroom Spinach Farfalle

Preparation time: 15 minutes
Cook time: 15 minutes
Servings: 2

Ingredients:

- 6 oz whole wheat farfalle (bowtie) pasta
- 2 cups sliced mushrooms
- 2 cups baby spinach
- 2 cloves garlic, minced
- 2 tablespoons extra virgin olive oil
- 1/4 cup grated Pecorino Romano cheese
- Salt and pepper to taste

Instructions:

1. Cook whole wheat farfalle pasta according to package instructions. Drain and set aside.
2. In a large skillet, heat olive oil over medium heat.
3. Add minced garlic and sauté for about 1 minute, until fragrant.
4. Add sliced mushrooms to the skillet and sauté for about 4-5 minutes, until they release their moisture and are slightly browned.
5. Add baby spinach to the skillet and cook until wilted.
6. Toss cooked farfalle pasta into the skillet and mix well.
7. Season with salt and pepper to taste.
8. Divide the pasta between two plates.
9. Sprinkle grated Pecorino Romano cheese over the pasta.
10. Serve the mushroom spinach farfalle as a wholesome and earthy dish.

Nutritional Information (per serving):
Cal: 370 | Carbs: 50g | Pro: 13g | Fat: 13g | Sugars: 3g | Fiber: 8g | Sodium: 360mg

9. Artichoke Lemon Linguine

Preparation time: 10 minutes
Cook time: 15 minutes
Servings: 2

Ingredients:

- 6 oz whole wheat linguine
- 1 cup artichoke hearts, chopped
- Juice and zest of 1 lemon
- 2 cloves garlic, minced
- 2 tablespoons extra virgin olive oil
- 1/4 cup chopped fresh parsley
- Salt and pepper to taste

Instructions:

1. Cook whole wheat linguine according to package instructions. Drain and set aside.
2. In a skillet, heat olive oil over medium heat.
3. Add minced garlic and sauté for about 1 minute, until fragrant.
4. Add chopped artichoke hearts to the skillet and sauté for about 2-3 minutes.
5. Toss cooked linguine into the skillet.
6. Stir in lemon juice and zest, and chopped fresh parsley.
7. Season with salt and pepper to taste.
8. Divide the pasta between two plates.
9. Serve the artichoke lemon linguine as a zesty and delightful dish.

Nutritional Information (per serving):
Cal: 340 | Carbs: 49g | Pro: 10g | Fat: 11g | Sugars: 4g | Fiber: 7g | Sodium: 250mg

10. Eggplant Tomato Rotini

Preparation time: 20 minutes
Cook time: 20 minutes
Servings: 2

Ingredients:

- 6 oz whole wheat rotini pasta
- 1 medium eggplant, diced
- 1 cup diced tomatoes
- 2 cloves garlic, minced
- 2 tablespoons extra virgin olive oil
- 1/4 cup grated Parmesan cheese
- Salt and pepper to taste

Instructions:

1. Cook whole wheat rotini pasta according to package instructions. Drain and set aside.
2. In a skillet, heat olive oil over medium heat.
3. Add minced garlic and sauté for about 1 minute, until fragrant.
4. Add diced eggplant to the skillet and sauté for about 5-6 minutes, until slightly softened.
5. Add diced tomatoes to the skillet and cook for another 2-3 minutes.
6. Toss cooked rotini pasta into the skillet and mix well.
7. Season with salt and pepper to taste.
8. Divide the pasta between two plates.
9. Sprinkle grated Parmesan cheese over the pasta.
10. Serve the eggplant tomato rotini as a hearty and satisfying dish.

Nutritional Information (per serving):
Cal: 380 | Carbs: 57g | Pro: 13g | Fat: 13g | Sugars: 7g | Fiber: 10g | Sodium: 330mg

11. Asparagus Pesto Spaghetti

Preparation time: 15 minutes
Cook time: 15 minutes
Servings: 2

Ingredients:

- 6 oz whole wheat spaghetti
- 1 cup asparagus spears, chopped
- 1/4 cup pine nuts
- 2 cloves garlic, minced
- 2 cups fresh basil leaves
- 1/4 cup grated Parmesan cheese
- 3 tablespoons extra virgin olive oil
- Salt and pepper to taste

Instructions:

1. Cook whole wheat spaghetti according to package instructions. Drain and set aside.
2. In a skillet, lightly toast pine nuts over medium heat until golden.
3. In a food processor, combine toasted pine nuts, minced garlic, fresh basil leaves, grated Parmesan cheese, and extra virgin olive oil. Blend until smooth.
4. In the same skillet, sauté chopped asparagus for about 3-4 minutes, until tender.
5. Toss cooked spaghetti with the asparagus pesto sauce.
6. Season with salt and pepper to taste.
7. Divide the pasta between two plates.
8. Serve the asparagus pesto spaghetti as a vibrant and flavorful dish.

Nutritional Information (per serving):
Cal: 410 | Carbs: 42g | Pro: 12g | Fat: 23g | Sugars: 2g | Fiber: 8g | Sodium: 220mg

12. Tuna Olive Orecchiette

Preparation time: 15 minutes
Cook time: 15 minutes
Servings: 2

Ingredients:

- 6 oz whole wheat orecchiette pasta
- 1 can (5 oz) tuna, drained and flaked
- 1/4 cup sliced Kalamata olives
- 1/4 cup diced red onion
- 2 tablespoons capers
- 2 tablespoons extra virgin olive oil
- Juice of 1 lemon
- Salt and pepper to taste

Instructions:

1. Cook whole wheat orecchiette pasta according

to package instructions. Drain and set aside.
2. In a bowl, combine drained and flaked tuna, sliced Kalamata olives, diced red onion, capers, extra virgin olive oil, and lemon juice.
3. Toss cooked orecchiette pasta with the tuna and olive mixture.
4. Season with salt and pepper to taste.
5. Divide the pasta between two plates.
6. Serve the tuna olive orecchiette as a protein-packed and zesty dish.

Nutritional Information (per serving):
Cal: 380 | Carbs: 45g | Pro: 20g | Fat: 14g | Sugars: 3g | Fiber: 7g | Sodium: 520mg

13. Roasted Red Pepper Penne

Preparation time: 15 minutes
Cook time: 20 minutes
Servings: 2

Ingredients:

- 6 oz whole wheat penne pasta
- 1 cup roasted red bell peppers, sliced
- 1/2 cup diced red onion
- 2 cloves garlic, minced
- 2 tablespoons extra virgin olive oil
- 1/4 cup crumbled goat cheese
- 2 tablespoons chopped fresh basil
- Salt and pepper to taste

Instructions:

1. Cook whole wheat penne pasta according to package instructions. Drain and set aside.
2. In a skillet, heat olive oil over medium heat.
3. Add minced garlic and sauté for about 1 minute, until fragrant.
4. Add sliced roasted red bell peppers and diced red onion to the skillet. Sauté for about 3-4 minutes.
5. Toss cooked penne pasta into the skillet and mix well.
6. Season with salt and pepper to taste.
7. Divide the pasta between two plates.
8. Sprinkle crumbled goat cheese and chopped fresh basil over the pasta.
9. Serve the roasted red pepper penne as a flavorful and colorful dish.

Nutritional Information (per serving):
Cal: 370 | Carbs: 49g | Pro: 10g | Fat: 14g | Sugars: 7g | Fiber: 8g | Sodium: 280mg

14. Mediterranean Lentil Fusilli

Preparation time: 15 minutes
Cook time: 20 minutes
Servings: 2

Ingredients:

- 6 oz whole wheat fusilli pasta
- 1/2 cup cooked green lentils
- 1 cup diced cucumbers
- 1/2 cup diced tomatoes
- 2 tablespoons chopped fresh parsley
- 2 tablespoons extra virgin olive oil
- Juice of 1 lemon
- Salt and pepper to taste

Instructions:

1. Cook whole wheat fusilli pasta according to package instructions. Drain and set aside.
2. In a bowl, combine cooked green lentils, diced cucumbers, diced tomatoes, chopped fresh parsley, extra virgin olive oil, and lemon juice.
3. Toss cooked fusilli pasta with the lentil and vegetable mixture.
4. Season with salt and pepper to taste.
5. Divide the pasta between two plates.
6. Serve the Mediterranean lentil fusilli as a protein-rich and refreshing dish.

Nutritional Information (per serving):
Cal: 360 | Carbs: 54g | Pro: 13g | Fat: 10g | Sugars: 4g | Fiber: 10g | Sodium: 320mg

15. Sundried Tomato Gemelli

Preparation time: 15 minutes
Cook time: 15 minutes
Servings: 2

Ingredients:

- 6 oz whole wheat gemelli pasta
- 1/4 cup sundried tomatoes, chopped
- 1/4 cup chopped Kalamata olives
- 2 cloves garlic, minced
- 2 tablespoons extra virgin olive oil
- 2 tablespoons chopped fresh basil
- Salt and pepper to taste

Instructions:

1. Cook whole wheat gemelli pasta according to package instructions. Drain and set aside.
2. In a skillet, heat olive oil over medium heat.
3. Add minced garlic and sauté for about 1 minute, until fragrant.
4. Add chopped sundried tomatoes and chopped Kalamata olives to the skillet. Sauté for about 2-3 minutes.
5. Toss cooked gemelli pasta into the skillet and mix well.
6. Season with salt and pepper to taste.
7. Divide the pasta between two plates.
8. Sprinkle chopped fresh basil over the pasta.
9. Serve the sundried tomato gemelli as a flavorful

and tangy dish.

Nutritional Information (per serving):
Cal: 350 | Carbs: 53g | Pro: 9g | Fat: 12g | Sugars: 4g | Fiber: 7g | Sodium: 360mg

16. Lemon Garlic Angel Hair

Preparation time: 15 minutes
Cook time: 10 minutes
Servings: 2

Ingredients:

- 6 oz whole wheat angel hair pasta
- 2 tablespoons extra virgin olive oil
- 2 cloves garlic, minced
- Zest and juice of 1 lemon
- 2 tablespoons chopped fresh parsley
- Salt and pepper to taste

Instructions:

1. Cook whole wheat angel hair pasta according to package instructions. Drain and set aside.
2. In a skillet, heat olive oil over medium heat.
3. Add minced garlic and sauté for about 1 minute, until fragrant.
4. Remove the skillet from heat and add lemon zest and juice. Mix well.
5. Toss cooked angel hair pasta into the skillet and coat with the lemon garlic mixture.
6. Season with salt and pepper to taste.
7. Divide the pasta between two plates.
8. Sprinkle chopped fresh parsley over the pasta.
9. Serve the lemon garlic angel hair as a simple and zesty dish.

Nutritional Information (per serving):
Cal: 320 | Carbs: 50g | Pro: 9g | Fat: 11g | Sugars: 2g | Fiber: 7g | Sodium: 230mg

17. Broccoli Walnut Rigatoni

Preparation time: 15 minutes
Cook time: 15 minutes
Servings: 2

Ingredients:

- 6 oz whole wheat rigatoni pasta
- 2 cups broccoli florets
- 1/4 cup chopped walnuts
- 2 cloves garlic, minced
- 2 tablespoons extra virgin olive oil
- 1/4 cup grated Parmesan cheese
- Salt and pepper to taste

Instructions:

1. Cook whole wheat rigatoni pasta according to package instructions. Drain and set aside.
2. Steam broccoli florets until tender.
3. In a skillet, heat olive oil over medium heat.
4. Add minced garlic and sauté for about 1 minute, until fragrant.
5. Add steamed broccoli florets and chopped walnuts to the skillet. Sauté for about 3-4 minutes.
6. Toss cooked rigatoni pasta into the skillet and mix well.
7. Season with salt and pepper to taste.
8. Divide the pasta between two plates.
9. Sprinkle grated Parmesan cheese over the pasta.
10. Serve the broccoli walnut rigatoni as a hearty and nutritious dish.

Nutritional Information (per serving):
Cal: 380 | Carbs: 47g | Pro: 14g | Fat: 17g | Sugars: 3g | Fiber: 8g | Sodium: 270mg

18. Zesty Shrimp Linguine

Preparation time: 15 minutes
Cook time: 10 minutes
Servings: 2

Ingredients:

- 6 oz whole wheat linguine
- 8 oz shrimp, peeled and deveined
- 2 cloves garlic, minced
- 2 tablespoons extra virgin olive oil
- 1/4 teaspoon red pepper flakes
- Juice of 1 lemon
- 2 tablespoons chopped fresh parsley
- Salt and pepper to taste

Instructions:

1. Cook whole wheat linguine according to package instructions. Drain and set aside.
2. In a skillet, heat olive oil over medium heat.
3. Add minced garlic and red pepper flakes. Sauté for about 1 minute.
4. Add shrimp to the skillet and cook for about 2-3 minutes on each side, until pink and opaque.
5. Remove the skillet from heat and add lemon juice. Mix well.
6. Toss cooked linguine with the zesty shrimp mixture.
7. Season with salt and pepper to taste.
8. Divide the pasta between two plates.
9. Sprinkle chopped fresh parsley over the pasta.
10. Serve the zesty shrimp linguine as a protein-packed and flavorful dish.

Nutritional Information (per serving):
Cal: 350 | Carbs: 47g | Pro: 24g | Fat: 9g | Sugars: 2g | Fiber: 7g | Sodium: 320mg

19. Spinach Walnut Farfalle

Preparation time: 15 minutes
Cook time: 15 minutes
Servings: 2

Ingredients:

- 6 oz whole wheat farfalle (bowtie) pasta
- 4 cups baby spinach
- 1/4 cup chopped walnuts
- 2 cloves garlic, minced
- 2 tablespoons extra virgin olive oil
- 1/4 cup grated Pecorino Romano cheese
- Salt and pepper to taste

Instructions:

1. Cook whole wheat farfalle pasta according to package instructions. Drain and set aside.
2. In a large skillet, heat olive oil over medium heat.
3. Add minced garlic and sauté for about 1 minute, until fragrant.
4. Add baby spinach to the skillet and sauté until wilted.
5. Toss cooked farfalle pasta into the skillet and mix well.
6. Stir in chopped walnuts.
7. Season with salt and pepper to taste.
8. Divide the pasta between two plates.
9. Sprinkle grated Pecorino Romano cheese over the pasta.
10. Serve the spinach walnut farfalle as a nourishing and nutty dish.

Nutritional Information (per serving):
Cal: 360 | Carbs: 45g | Pro: 12g | Fat: 15g | Sugars: 2g | Fiber: 7g | Sodium: 280mg

20. Mediterranean Pesto Bowls

Preparation time: 15 minutes
Cook time: 15 minutes
Servings: 2

Ingredients:

- 6 oz whole wheat bowtie pasta
- 1 cup diced cucumber
- 1 cup diced tomatoes
- 1/2 cup chopped Kalamata olives
- 1/4 cup crumbled feta cheese
- 2 tablespoons chopped fresh basil
- 2 tablespoons extra virgin olive oil
- Salt and pepper to taste

Instructions:

1. Cook whole wheat bowtie pasta according to package instructions. Drain and set aside.

2. In a bowl, combine diced cucumber, diced tomatoes, chopped Kalamata olives, crumbled feta cheese, chopped fresh basil, and extra virgin olive oil.
3. Toss cooked bowtie pasta with the Mediterranean vegetable mixture.
4. Season with salt and pepper to taste.
5. Divide the pasta between two bowls.
6. Serve the Mediterranean pesto bowls as a refreshing and satisfying dish.

Nutritional Information (per serving):
Cal: 380 | Carbs: 51g | Pro: 11g | Fat: 15g | Sugars: 5g | Fiber: 8g | Sodium: 430mg

Main Courses

1. Grilled Salmon Skewers

Preparation time: 15 minutes
Cook time: 10 minutes
Servings: 2

Ingredients:

- 2 salmon fillets, cut into chunks
- 1 red bell pepper, cut into chunks
- 1 red onion, cut into chunks
- 2 tablespoons extra virgin olive oil
- Juice of 1 lemon
- 2 teaspoons dried oregano
- Salt and pepper to taste

Instructions:

1. Preheat the grill to medium-high heat.
2. Thread salmon chunks, red bell pepper, and red onion onto skewers.
3. In a bowl, whisk together olive oil, lemon juice, dried oregano, salt, and pepper.
4. Brush the marinade over the skewers.
5. Grill the skewers for about 4-5 minutes on each side, until salmon is cooked through.
6. Remove from the grill and serve.

Nutritional Information (per serving):
Cal: 320 | Carbs: 8g | Pro: 30g | Fat: 20g | Sugars: 4g | Fiber: 2g | Sodium: 170mg

2. Lemon Herb Chicken

Preparation time: 10 minutes
Cook time: 20 minutes
Servings: 2

Ingredients:

- 2 boneless, skinless chicken breasts
- Juice of 1 lemon
- 2 tablespoons chopped fresh rosemary
- 2 cloves garlic, minced
- 2 tablespoons extra virgin olive oil
- Salt and pepper to taste

Instructions:

1. Preheat the oven to 400°F (200°C).
2. In a bowl, mix together lemon juice, chopped rosemary, minced garlic, olive oil, salt, and pepper.
3. Place chicken breasts in a baking dish and pour the marinade over them.
4. Bake for about 20 minutes, until chicken is cooked through.
5. Serve the lemon herb chicken with a side of vegetables.

Nutritional Information (per serving):
Cal: 260 | Carbs: 4g | Pro: 30g | Fat: 14g | Sugars: 1g | Fiber: 1g | Sodium: 130mg

3. Mediterranean Stuffed Peppers

Preparation time: 15 minutes
Cook time: 30 minutes
Servings: 2

Ingredients:

- 2 large bell peppers, halved and seeds removed
- 1 cup cooked quinoa
- 1 cup canned chickpeas, drained and rinsed
- 1/2 cup diced tomatoes
- 2 tablespoons chopped fresh parsley
- 2 tablespoons crumbled feta cheese
- Salt and pepper to taste

Instructions:

1. Preheat the oven to 375°F (190°C).
2. In a bowl, mix cooked quinoa, chickpeas, diced tomatoes, chopped parsley, crumbled feta cheese, salt, and pepper.
3. Fill the bell pepper halves with the quinoa mixture.
4. Place stuffed peppers in a baking dish and cover with aluminum foil.
5. Bake for about 25-30 minutes, until peppers are tender.
6. Serve the Mediterranean stuffed peppers as a wholesome main course.

Nutritional Information (per serving):
Cal: 320 | Carbs: 49g | Pro: 14g | Fat: 7g | Sugars: 8g | Fiber: 12g | Sodium: 480mg

4. Balsamic Glazed Pork

Preparation time: 10 minutes
Cook time: 20 minutes
Servings: 2

Ingredients:

- 2 boneless pork chops
- 2 tablespoons balsamic vinegar
- 2 tablespoons honey
- 2 cloves garlic, minced
- 2 tablespoons chopped fresh thyme
- Salt and pepper to taste

Instructions:

1. Preheat a skillet over medium-high heat.
2. Season pork chops with salt and pepper.
3. In a bowl, whisk together balsamic vinegar, honey, minced garlic, and chopped thyme.
4. Add pork chops to the skillet and pour the balsa

mic mixture over them.

5. Cook pork chops for about 4-5 minutes on each side, until cooked through and glazed.
6. Serve the balsamic glazed pork with a side of vegetables.

Nutritional Information (per serving):
Cal: 300 | Carbs: 16g | Pro: 28g | Fat: 14g | Sugars: 14g | Fiber: 0g | Sodium: 220mg

5. Shrimp and Orzo Salad

Preparation time: 15 minutes
Cook time: 10 minutes
Servings: 2

Ingredients:

- 8 oz shrimp, peeled and deveined
- 1 cup cooked whole wheat orzo
- 1 cup cherry tomatoes, halved
- 1/4 cup diced red onion
- 2 tablespoons chopped fresh dill
- 2 tablespoons extra virgin olive oil
- Juice of 1 lemon
- Salt and pepper to taste

Instructions:

1. Season shrimp with salt and pepper.
2. In a skillet, heat olive oil over medium-high heat.
3. Add shrimp and cook for about 2-3 minutes on each side, until pink and opaque.
4. In a bowl, combine cooked orzo, cherry tomatoes, diced red onion, chopped dill, and cooked shrimp.
5. Drizzle with lemon juice and extra virgin olive oil.
6. Season with salt and pepper to taste.
7. Serve the shrimp and orzo salad as a refreshing main course.

Nutritional Information (per serving):
Cal: 340 | Carbs: 32g | Pro: 28g | Fat: 12g | Sugars: 3g | Fiber: 3g | Sodium: 250mg

6. Herb Crusted Whitefish

Preparation time: 10 minutes
Cook time: 15 minutes
Servings: 2

Ingredients:

- 2 whitefish fillets (such as cod or haddock)
- 1/4 cup whole wheat breadcrumbs
- 2 tablespoons chopped fresh parsley
- 2 tablespoons chopped fresh dill
- 2 tablespoons grated Parmesan cheese
- 2 tablespoons extra virgin olive oil
- Salt and pepper to taste

Instructions:

1. Preheat the oven to 400°F (200°C).
2. In a bowl, mix together whole wheat breadcrumbs, chopped parsley, chopped dill, grated Parmesan cheese, salt, and pepper.
3. Brush whitefish fillets with extra virgin olive oil.
4. Press the breadcrumb mixture onto the top of each fillet.
5. Place fillets on a baking sheet and bake for about 12-15 minutes, until fish flakes easily with a fork.
6. Serve the herb crusted whitefish with a side of steamed vegetables.

Nutritional Information (per serving):
Cal: 280 | Carbs: 12g | Pro: 30g | Fat: 13g | Sugars: 1g | Fiber: 2g | Sodium: 340mg

7. Greek Turkey Burgers

Preparation time: 15 minutes
Cook time: 12 minutes
Servings: 2

Ingredients:

- 1/2 lb lean ground turkey
- 1/4 cup chopped red onion
- 2 cloves garlic, minced
- 2 tablespoons chopped fresh oregano
- 2 tablespoons crumbled feta cheese
- Salt and pepper to taste

Instructions:

1. In a bowl, combine lean ground turkey, chopped red onion, minced garlic, chopped oregano, crumbled feta cheese, salt, and pepper.
2. Divide the mixture into two portions and shape into burger patties.
3. Preheat a skillet or grill pan over medium-high heat.
4. Cook the turkey burgers for about 5-6 minutes on each side, until cooked through.
5. Serve the Greek turkey burgers with a side of Greek salad.

Nutritional Information (per serving):
Cal: 220 | Carbs: 5g | Pro: 25g | Fat: 11g | Sugars: 2g | Fiber: 1g | Sodium: 240mg

8. Lentil Spinach Curry

Preparation time: 10 minutes
Cook time: 25 minutes
Servings: 2

Ingredients:

- 1 cup cooked green lentils

- 2 cups baby spinach
- 1 onion, chopped
- 2 cloves garlic, minced
- 1 tablespoon olive oil
- 1 teaspoon curry powder
- 1/2 teaspoon ground cumin
- Salt and pepper to taste

Instructions:

1. In a skillet, heat olive oil over medium heat.
2. Add chopped onion and sauté for about 3-4 minutes, until softened.
3. Add minced garlic, curry powder, and ground cumin. Sauté for another minute.
4. Add cooked green lentils and baby spinach to the skillet. Cook until spinach is wilted.
5. Season with salt and pepper to taste.
6. Serve the lentil spinach curry as a flavorful and nutritious main course.

Nutritional Information (per serving):
Cal: 250 | Carbs: 37g | Pro: 14g | Fat: 5g | Sugars: 4g | Fiber: 14g | Sodium: 250mg

9. Tomato Basil Cod

Preparation time: 10 minutes
Cook time: 20 minutes
Servings: 2

Ingredients:

- 2 cod fillets
- 1 cup diced tomatoes
- 1/4 cup chopped fresh basil
- 2 cloves garlic, minced
- 2 tablespoons extra virgin olive oil
- Salt and pepper to taste

Instructions:

1. Preheat the oven to 375°F (190°C).
2. In a bowl, mix together diced tomatoes, chopped basil, minced garlic, extra virgin olive oil, salt, and pepper.
3. Place cod fillets in a baking dish and spoon the tomato basil mixture over them.
4. Bake for about 15-20 minutes, until cod is opaque and flakes easily.
5. Serve the tomato basil cod with a side of whole wheat couscous.

Nutritional Information (per serving):
Cal: 280 | Carbs: 7g | Pro: 27g | Fat: 15g | Sugars: 3g | Fiber: 2g | Sodium: 220mg

10. Chickpea Spinach Stew

Preparation time: 10 minutes

Cook time: 25 minutes
Servings: 2

Ingredients:

- 1 can (15 oz) chickpeas, drained and rinsed
- 2 cups baby spinach
- 1 onion, chopped
- 2 cloves garlic, minced
- 2 tablespoons extra virgin olive oil
- 1 teaspoon ground cumin
- 1/2 teaspoon smoked paprika
- Salt and pepper to taste

Instructions:

1. In a skillet, heat olive oil over medium heat.
2. Add chopped onion and sauté for about 3-4 minutes, until softened.
3. Add minced garlic, ground cumin, and smoked paprika. Sauté for another minute.
4. Add chickpeas and baby spinach to the skillet. Cook until spinach is wilted and chickpeas are heated through.
5. Season with salt and pepper to taste.
6. Serve the chickpea spinach stew as a comforting and protein-packed dish.

Nutritional Information (per serving):
Cal: 290 | Carbs: 36g | Pro: 12g | Fat: 12g | Sugars: 7g | Fiber: 10g | Sodium: 490mg

11. Citrus Marinated Swordfish

Preparation time: 10 minutes
Cook time: 10 minutes
Servings: 2

Ingredients:

- 2 swordfish steaks
- Juice of 1 orange
- Juice of 1 lemon
- 2 cloves garlic, minced
- 2 tablespoons chopped fresh thyme
- 2 tablespoons extra virgin olive oil
- Salt and pepper to taste

Instructions:

1. In a bowl, combine orange juice, lemon juice, minced garlic, chopped thyme, extra virgin olive oil, salt, and pepper.
2. Place swordfish steaks in a shallow dish and pour the marinade over them.
3. Marinate for about 15-20 minutes.
4. Preheat a grill or skillet over medium-high heat.
5. Cook swordfish steaks for about 4-5 minutes on each side, until cooked through.
6. Serve the citrus marinated swordfish with a side of quinoa.

Nutritional Information (per serving):
Cal: 320 | Carbs: 10g | Pro: 35g | Fat: 15g | Sugars: 5g | Fiber: 1g | Sodium: 300mg

12. Zucchini Noodle Primavera

Preparation time: 15 minutes
Cook time: 10 minutes
Servings: 2

Ingredients:

- 2 medium zucchinis, spiralized into noodles
- 1 cup cherry tomatoes, halved
- 1 cup sliced bell peppers
- 2 cloves garlic, minced
- 2 tablespoons chopped fresh basil
- 2 tablespoons extra virgin olive oil
- Grated Parmesan cheese for topping
- Salt and pepper to taste

Instructions:

1. In a skillet, heat olive oil over medium heat.
2. Add minced garlic and sauté for about 1 minute, until fragrant.
3. Add cherry tomatoes and sliced bell peppers. Cook for about 2-3 minutes.
4. Add zucchini noodles to the skillet and cook for another 2 minutes, until tender.
5. Toss in chopped basil and season with salt and pepper.
6. Divide the zucchini noodle primavera between two plates.
7. Sprinkle grated Parmesan cheese over the noodles.
8. Serve as a light and veggie-packed main course.

Nutritional Information (per serving):
Cal: 180 | Carbs: 14g | Pro: 4g | Fat: 13g | Sugars: 8g | Fiber: 4g | Sodium: 110mg

13. Olive Roasted Chicken

Preparation time: 10 minutes
Cook time: 25 minutes
Servings: 2

Ingredients:

- 2 boneless chicken breasts
- 1/4 cup pitted Kalamata olives
- 2 tablespoons chopped fresh rosemary
- 2 tablespoons chopped fresh thyme
- 2 tablespoons extra virgin olive oil
- Salt and pepper to taste

Instructions:

1. Preheat the oven to 400°F (200°C).
2. Place chicken breasts in a baking dish.
3. Scatter pitted Kalamata olives around the chicken.
4. Drizzle extra virgin olive oil over the chicken and olives.
5. Sprinkle chopped rosemary and thyme over the chicken.
6. Season with salt and pepper.
7. Bake for about 20-25 minutes, until chicken is cooked through.
8. Serve the olive roasted chicken with a side of whole grain couscous.

Nutritional Information (per serving):
Cal: 320 | Carbs: 4g | Pro: 34g | Fat: 18g | Sugars: 0g | Fiber: 1g | Sodium: 390mg

14. Quinoa Stuffed Eggplant

Preparation time: 15 minutes
Cook time: 30 minutes
Servings: 2

Ingredients:

- 1 large eggplant
- 1 cup cooked quinoa
- 1/2 cup diced tomatoes
- 1/4 cup diced red onion
- 2 tablespoons chopped fresh parsley
- 2 tablespoons crumbled feta cheese
- 2 tablespoons extra virgin olive oil
- Salt and pepper to taste

Instructions:

1. Preheat the oven to 375°F (190°C).
2. Cut the eggplant in half lengthwise and scoop out the flesh, leaving a shell.
3. Chop the eggplant flesh and sauté it in olive oil with diced tomatoes and red onion.
4. In a bowl, mix together sautéed eggplant, cooked quinoa, chopped parsley, crumbled feta cheese, salt, and pepper.
5. Fill the eggplant shells with the quinoa mixture.
6. Place the stuffed eggplants in a baking dish and cover with aluminum foil.
7. Bake for about 25-30 minutes, until eggplant is tender.
8. Serve the quinoa stuffed eggplant as a satisfying and flavorful dish.

Nutritional Information (per serving):
Cal: 330 | Carbs: 41g | Pro: 8g | Fat: 16g | Sugars: 6g | Fiber: 11g | Sodium: 270mg

15. Feta Crusted Salmon

Preparation time: 10 minutes
Cook time: 15 minutes

Servings: 2

Ingredients:

- 2 salmon fillets
- 1/4 cup crumbled feta cheese
- 2 tablespoons chopped fresh dill
- 2 tablespoons extra virgin olive oil
- Juice of 1 lemon
- Salt and pepper to taste

Instructions:

1. Preheat the oven to 375°F (190°C).
2. Place salmon fillets on a baking sheet.
3. In a bowl, mix together crumbled feta cheese, chopped dill, extra virgin olive oil, lemon juice, salt, and pepper.
4. Press the feta mixture onto the top of each salmon fillet.
5. Bake for about 12-15 minutes, until salmon is cooked through.
6. Serve the feta crusted salmon with a side of roasted vegetables.

Nutritional Information (per serving):
Cal: 300 | Carbs: 2g | Pro: 30g | Fat: 20g | Sugars: 1g | Fiber: 0g | Sodium: 300mg

16. Spinach Mushroom Frittata

Preparation time: 10 minutes
Cook time: 20 minutes
Servings: 2

Ingredients:

- 4 eggs
- 1 cup baby spinach
- 1 cup sliced mushrooms
- 1/4 cup diced onion
- 2 tablespoons grated Parmesan cheese
- 2 tablespoons extra virgin olive oil
- Salt and pepper to taste

Instructions:

1. Preheat the oven to 375°F (190°C).
2. In a skillet, heat olive oil over medium heat.
3. Add diced onion and sliced mushrooms. Cook for about 3-4 minutes.
4. Add baby spinach and sauté until wilted.
5. In a bowl, whisk together eggs, grated Parmesan cheese, salt, and pepper.
6. Pour the egg mixture over the sautéed vegetables in the skillet.
7. Cook on the stovetop for 3-4 minutes until the edges are set.
8. Transfer the skillet to the preheated oven and bake for another 10-12 minutes, until the frittata is fully set.

9. Slice the spinach mushroom frittata into wedges and serve.

Nutritional Information (per serving):
Cal: 250 | Carbs: 7g | Pro: 15g | Fat: 18g | Sugars: 2g | Fiber: 2g | Sodium: 350mg

17. Greek Yogurt Marinated Chicken

Preparation time: 10 minutes
Cook time: 15 minutes
Servings: 2

Ingredients:

- 2 boneless chicken breasts
- 1/2 cup Greek yogurt
- 2 tablespoons chopped fresh oregano
- 2 cloves garlic, minced
- 2 tablespoons lemon juice
- 1 tablespoon extra virgin olive oil
- Salt and pepper to taste

Instructions:

1. In a bowl, mix together Greek yogurt, chopped oregano, minced garlic, lemon juice, extra virgin olive oil, salt, and pepper.
2. Place chicken breasts in the marinade and coat them well.
3. Marinate for about 20-30 minutes.
4. Preheat a grill or skillet over medium-high heat.
5. Cook chicken breasts for about 6-7 minutes on each side, until cooked through.
6. Serve the Greek yogurt marinated chicken with a side of roasted potatoes.

Nutritional Information (per serving):
Cal: 260 | Carbs: 7g | Pro: 30g | Fat: 13g | Sugars: 3g | Fiber: 1g | Sodium: 250mg

18. Mediterranean Tofu Stir Fry

Preparation time: 15 minutes
Cook time: 15 minutes
Servings: 2

Ingredients:

- 8 oz extra firm tofu, cubed
- 1 cup sliced bell peppers
- 1 cup sliced zucchini
- 2 cloves garlic, minced
- 2 tablespoons low-sodium soy sauce
- 2 tablespoons extra virgin olive oil
- 1 tablespoon chopped fresh basil
- Salt and pepper to taste

Instructions:

1. In a skillet, heat olive oil over medium-high heat.
2. Add cubed tofu and cook until golden brown on all sides.
3. Add sliced bell peppers and sliced zucchini. Cook for about 3-4 minutes.
4. Add minced garlic and sauté for another minute.
5. Pour in low-sodium soy sauce and toss to coat.
6. Season with salt, pepper, and chopped basil.
7. Serve the Mediterranean tofu stir-fry over a bed of cooked quinoa.

Nutritional Information (per serving):
Cal: 320 | Carbs: 18g | Pro: 18g | Fat: 20g | Sugars: 6g | Fiber: 5g | Sodium: 520mg

19. Baked Cod with Tomatoes

Preparation time: 10 minutes
Cook time: 20 minutes
Servings: 2

Ingredients:

- 2 cod fillets
- 1 cup diced tomatoes
- 2 cloves garlic, minced
- 2 tablespoons chopped fresh parsley
- 2 tablespoons extra virgin olive oil
- Juice of 1 lemon
- Salt and pepper to taste

Instructions:

1. Preheat the oven to 375°F (190°C).
2. Place cod fillets in a baking dish.
3. In a bowl, mix together diced tomatoes, minced garlic, chopped parsley, extra virgin olive oil, lemon juice, salt, and pepper.
4. Spoon the tomato mixture over the cod fillets.
5. Bake for about 15-20 minutes, until cod is cooked through.
6. Serve the baked cod with tomatoes over a bed of cooked brown rice.

Nutritional Information (per serving):
Cal: 250 | Carbs: 8g | Pro: 30g | Fat: 11g | Sugars: 4g | Fiber: 2g | Sodium: 300mg

20. Lemony Garlic Shrimp

Preparation time: 10 minutes
Cook time: 10 minutes
Servings: 2

Ingredients:

- 8 oz shrimp, peeled and deveined
- 2 cloves garlic, minced
- 2 tablespoons chopped fresh parsley
- 2 tablespoons extra virgin olive oil
- Juice of 1 lemon
- Salt and pepper to taste

Instructions:

1. In a bowl, mix together minced garlic, chopped parsley, extra virgin olive oil, lemon juice, salt, and pepper.
2. Season shrimp with the garlic mixture.
3. Preheat a skillet over medium-high heat.
4. Add shrimp and cook for about 2-3 minutes on each side, until pink and opaque.
5. Serve the lemony garlic shrimp with a side of whole wheat couscous.

Nutritional Information (per serving):
Cal: 220 | Carbs: 7g | Pro: 20g | Fat: 12g | Sugars: 1g | Fiber: 1g | Sodium: 250mg

Soups

1. Lentil Veggie Soup

Preparation time: 15 minutes
Servings: 2

Ingredients:

- 1/2 cup dried green lentils, rinsed
- 2 cups vegetable broth
- 1 carrot, diced
- 1 celery stalk, diced
- 1/2 onion, diced
- 1 teaspoon olive oil
- Salt and pepper to taste

Instructions:

1. In a pot, heat olive oil over medium heat.
2. Add diced onion, carrot, and celery. Sauté until slightly softened.
3. Add lentils and vegetable broth.
4. Bring to a boil, then reduce heat and simmer for 20-25 minutes, or until lentils are tender.
5. Season with salt and pepper.
6. Serve the lentil veggie soup warm.

Nutritional Information (per serving):
Cal: 220 | Carbs: 38g | Pro: 14g | Fat: 2g | Sugars: 6g | Fiber: 15g | Sodium: 900mg

2. Tomato Basil Bisque

Preparation time: 20 minutes
Servings: 2

Ingredients:

- 1 can (14 oz) diced tomatoes
- 1/2 cup chopped fresh basil
- 1/2 onion, diced
- 1 garlic clove, minced
- 1 tablespoon olive oil
- 1/2 cup low-sodium vegetable broth
- Salt and pepper to taste

Instructions:

1. In a pot, heat olive oil over medium heat.
2. Add diced onion and garlic. Sauté until onion is translucent.
3. Add diced tomatoes (with juices) and chopped basil.
4. Pour in vegetable broth and bring to a simmer.
5. Cook for about 10 minutes.
6. Use an immersion blender to blend the soup until smooth.
7. Season with salt and pepper.
8. Serve the tomato basil bisque hot.

Nutritional Information (per serving):
Cal: 150 | Carbs: 18g | Pro: 3g | Fat: 7g | Sugars: 10g | Fiber: 4g | Sodium: 450mg

3. Spinach Chickpea Soup

Preparation time: 20 minutes
Servings: 2

Ingredients:

- 1 can (15 oz) chickpeas, drained and rinsed
- 2 cups low-sodium vegetable broth
- 2 cups fresh spinach leaves
- 1 carrot, diced
- 1/2 onion, diced
- 1 tablespoon olive oil
- Salt and pepper to taste

Instructions:

1. In a pot, heat olive oil over medium heat.
2. Add diced onion and carrot. Sauté until softened.
3. Add chickpeas and vegetable broth.
4. Simmer for about 10 minutes.
5. Stir in fresh spinach until wilted.
6. Use an immersion blender to slightly blend the soup, leaving some chunks.
7. Season with salt and pepper.
8. Serve the spinach chickpea soup warm.

Nutritional Information (per serving):
Cal: 240 | Carbs: 38g | Pro: 11g | Fat: 6g | Sugars: 6g | Fiber: 10g | Sodium: 900mg

4. Greek Lemon Chicken

Preparation time: 25 minutes
Servings: 2

Ingredients:

- 2 boneless, skinless chicken breasts
- 4 cups low-sodium chicken broth
- 1 lemon, juiced and zested
- 1/2 cup orzo pasta
- 1/2 onion, diced
- 1 garlic clove, minced
- Fresh dill (for garnish)
- Salt and pepper to taste

Instructions:

1. In a pot, bring chicken broth to a simmer.
2. Add diced onion and minced garlic. Cook until onion is translucent.
3. Add chicken breasts and cook for about 15-20 minutes, until cooked through.
4. Remove chicken, shred it, and return to the pot.

5. Add orzo pasta and cook until tender.
6. Stir in lemon juice and zest.
7. Season with salt and pepper.
8. Garnish with fresh dill.
9. Serve the Greek lemon chicken soup hot.

Nutritional Information (per serving):
Cal: 310 | Carbs: 29g | Pro: 30g | Fat: 7g | Sugars: 5g | Fiber: 3g | Sodium: 500mg

5. Minestrone Delight

Preparation time: 25 minutes
Servings: 2

Ingredients:

- 4 cups low-sodium vegetable broth
- 1/2 cup diced carrots
- 1/2 cup diced zucchini
- 1/2 cup diced celery
- 1/2 cup diced onion
- 1/2 cup whole wheat pasta (e.g., macaroni)
- 1 can (14 oz) diced tomatoes
- 1 teaspoon olive oil

Instructions:

1. In a pot, heat olive oil over medium heat.
2. Add diced onion, carrot, celery, and zucchini. Sauté until slightly softened.
3. Add vegetable broth and bring to a simmer.
4. Stir in diced tomatoes and pasta.
5. Cook until pasta is al dente, following package instructions.
6. Season with salt and pepper.
7. Serve the minestrone delight hot.

Nutritional Information (per serving):
Cal: 250 | Carbs: 48g | Pro: 8g | Fat: 3g | Sugars: 10g | Fiber: 8g | Sodium: 800mg

6. Roasted Red Pepper

Preparation time: 30 minutes
Servings: 2

Ingredients:

- 2 red bell peppers
- 2 cups low-sodium vegetable broth
- 1/2 onion, diced
- 1 garlic clove, minced
- 1 teaspoon olive oil
- 2 tablespoons Greek yogurt (for garnish)
- Fresh parsley (for garnish)
- Salt and pepper to taste

Instructions:

1. Preheat the oven to broil.
2. Place red bell peppers on a baking sheet and broil, turning occasionally, until charred.
3. Transfer peppers to a bowl, cover with plastic wrap, and let them steam for 10 minutes.
4. Peel, seed, and chop the roasted peppers.
5. In a pot, heat olive oil over medium heat.
6. Add diced onion and minced garlic. Cook until onion is translucent.
7. Add chopped roasted peppers and vegetable broth.
8. Simmer for about 10 minutes.
9. Use an immersion blender to blend the soup until smooth.
10. Season with salt and pepper.
11. Serve the roasted red pepper soup hot, topped with a dollop of Greek yogurt and fresh parsley.

Nutritional Information (per serving):
Cal: 150 | Carbs: 28g | Pro: 5g | Fat: 4g | Sugars: 14g | Fiber: 7g | Sodium: 700mg

7. Zucchini Herb Soup

Preparation time: 20 minutes
Servings: 2

Ingredients:

- 2 medium zucchinis, diced
- 4 cups low-sodium vegetable broth
- 1/2 onion, diced
- 1 garlic clove, minced
- 1 tablespoon olive oil
- 1 tablespoon chopped fresh herbs (e.g., basil, parsley)
- Salt and pepper to taste

Instructions:

1. In a pot, heat olive oil over medium heat.
2. Add diced onion and minced garlic. Sauté until onion is translucent.
3. Add diced zucchini and vegetable broth.
4. Simmer for about 10 minutes, until zucchini is tender.
5. Use an immersion blender to blend the soup until smooth.
6. Season with salt and pepper.
7. Stir in chopped fresh herbs.
8. Serve the zucchini herb soup hot.

Nutritional Information (per serving):
Cal: 110 | Carbs: 16g | Pro: 5g | Fat: 4g | Sugars: 9g | Fiber: 3g | Sodium: 700mg

8. Seafood Chowder

Preparation time: 30 minutes
Servings: 2

Ingredients:

- 4 cups low-sodium seafood or fish broth
- 1/2 cup diced potatoes
- 1/2 cup diced carrots
- 1/2 cup diced celery
- 1/2 cup diced onion
- 4 ounces white fish fillets (e.g., cod), diced
- 1/4 cup Greek yogurt
- Fresh dill (for garnish)
- Salt and pepper to taste

Instructions:

1. In a pot, bring seafood broth to a simmer.
2. Add diced potato, carrot, celery, and onion.
3. Simmer for about 15 minutes, until vegetables are tender.
4. Stir in diced white fish and cook for another 5 minutes, until fish is cooked through.
5. Season with salt and pepper.
6. Stir in Greek yogurt to make the chowder creamy.
7. Garnish with fresh dill.
8. Serve the seafood chowder hot.

Nutritional Information (per serving):
Cal: 270 | Carbs: 32g | Pro: 25g | Fat: 5g | Sugars: 9g | Fiber: 4g | Sodium: 900mg

9. Mediterranean Bean Soup

Preparation time: 25 minutes
Servings: 2

Ingredients:

- 2 cups low-sodium vegetable broth
- 1 can (15 oz) mixed beans, drained and rinsed
- 1/2 cup diced tomatoes
- 1/2 onion, diced
- 1 garlic clove, minced
- 1 tablespoon olive oil
- 1 teaspoon dried oregano
- Salt and pepper to taste

Instructions:

1. In a pot, heat olive oil over medium heat.
2. Add diced onion and minced garlic. Cook until onion is translucent.
3. Add diced tomatoes and mixed beans.
4. Pour in vegetable broth and bring to a simmer.
5. Stir in dried oregano.
6. Cook for about 10 minutes.
7. Season with salt and pepper.
8. Serve the Mediterranean bean soup warm.

Nutritional Information (per serving):
Cal: 250 | Carbs: 42g | Pro: 14g | Fat: 4g | Sugars: 6g | Fiber: 11g | Sodium: 900mg

10. Quinoa Vegetable Stew

Preparation time: 30 minutes
Servings: 2

Ingredients:

- 4 cups low-sodium vegetable broth
- 1/2 cup quinoa, rinsed
- 1 carrot, diced
- 1 celery stalk, diced
- 1/2 zucchini, diced
- 1/2 onion, diced
- 1 teaspoon olive oil
- Salt and pepper to taste

Instructions:

1. In a pot, heat olive oil over medium heat.
2. Add diced onion, carrot, celery, and zucchini. Sauté until slightly softened.
3. Add quinoa and vegetable broth.
4. Simmer for about 20 minutes, until quinoa is cooked and vegetables are tender.
5. Season with salt and pepper.
6. Serve the quinoa vegetable stew hot.

Nutritional Information (per serving):
Cal: 220 | Carbs: 40g | Pro: 6g | Fat: 3g | Sugars: 5g | Fiber: 6g | Sodium: 900mg

11. Cauliflower Curry Soup

Preparation time: 30 minutes
Servings: 2

Ingredients:

- 1 small cauliflower, chopped
- 4 cups low-sodium vegetable broth
- 1/2 onion, diced
- 1 garlic clove, minced
- 1 teaspoon curry powder
- 1 tablespoon olive oil
- 1/2 cup coconut milk
- Salt and pepper to taste

Instructions:

1. In a pot, heat olive oil over medium heat.
2. Add diced onion and minced garlic. Sauté until onion is translucent.
3. Add chopped cauliflower and curry powder. Cook for a few minutes.
4. Pour in vegetable broth and bring to a simmer.
5. Simmer for about 20 minutes, until cauliflower is tender.
6. Use an immersion blender to blend the soup until smooth.
7. Stir in coconut milk.

8. Season with salt and pepper.
9. Serve the cauliflower curry soup hot.

Nutritional Information (per serving):
Cal: 250 | Carbs: 20g | Pro: 5g | Fat: 18g | Sugars: 6g | Fiber: 6g | Sodium: 900mg

12. White Bean Rosemary

Preparation time: 25 minutes
Servings: 2

Ingredients:

- 1 can (15 oz) white beans, drained and rinsed
- 4 cups low-sodium vegetable broth
- 1/2 onion, diced
- 1 garlic clove, minced
- 1 tablespoon olive oil
- 1 teaspoon dried rosemary
- Salt and pepper to taste

Instructions:

1. In a pot, heat olive oil over medium heat.
2. Add diced onion and minced garlic. Sauté until onion is translucent.
3. Add drained white beans and vegetable broth.
4. Simmer for about 10 minutes.
5. Stir in dried rosemary.
6. Use an immersion blender to blend the soup slightly, leaving some beans whole.
7. Season with salt and pepper.
8. Serve the white bean rosemary soup warm.

Nutritional Information (per serving):
Cal: 220 | Carbs: 36g | Pro: 12g | Fat: 4g | Sugars: 3g | Fiber: 10g | Sodium: 900mg

13. Fisherman's Bouillabaisse

Preparation time: 30 minutes
Servings: 2

Ingredients:

- 4 cups low-sodium fish or seafood broth
- 1/2 cup diced potatoes
- 1/2 cup diced fennel
- 1/2 cup diced onion
- 4 ounces mixed seafood (shrimp, mussels, etc.)
- 1 tablespoon olive oil
- 1/2 teaspoon saffron threads
- Salt and pepper to taste

Instructions:

1. In a pot, heat olive oil over medium heat.
2. Add diced onion and fennel. Sauté until slightly softened.

3. Add diced potatoes and fish or seafood broth.
4. Simmer for about 15 minutes, until potatoes are tender.
5. Stir in mixed seafood and saffron threads.
6. Cook for another 5 minutes, until seafood is cooked through.
7. Season with salt and pepper.
8. Serve the Fisherman's bouillabaisse hot.

Nutritional Information (per serving):
Cal: 250 | Carbs: 26g | Pro: 20g | Fat: 8g | Sugars: 3g | Fiber: 4g | Sodium: 800mg

14. Broccoli Almond Soup

Preparation time: 20 minutes
Servings: 2

Ingredients:

- 2 cups chopped broccoli florets
- 4 cups low-sodium vegetable broth
- 1/2 onion, diced
- 1 garlic clove, minced
- 2 tablespoons almond butter
- 1 tablespoon olive oil
- Salt and pepper to taste

Instructions:

1. In a pot, heat olive oil over medium heat.
2. Add diced onion and minced garlic. Sauté until onion is translucent.
3. Add chopped broccoli and vegetable broth.
4. Simmer for about 10-15 minutes, until broccoli is tender.
5. Use an immersion blender to blend the soup until smooth.
6. Stir in almond butter until well combined.
7. Season with salt and pepper.
8. Serve the broccoli almond soup hot.

Nutritional Information (per serving):
Cal: 190 | Carbs: 18g | Pro: 8g | Fat: 12g | Sugars: 5g | Fiber: 5g | Sodium: 800mg

15. Eggplant Tomato Bisque

Preparation time: 30 minutes
Servings: 2

Ingredients:

- 1 medium eggplant, chopped
- 4 cups low-sodium vegetable broth
- 1/2 onion, diced
- 1 garlic clove, minced
- 1 can (14 oz) diced tomatoes
- 1 tablespoon olive oil
- 1/2 teaspoon dried basil

- Salt and pepper to taste

Instructions:

1. In a pot, heat olive oil over medium heat.
2. Add diced onion and minced garlic. Sauté until onion is translucent.
3. Add chopped eggplant and dried basil. Cook for a few minutes.
4. Pour in vegetable broth and bring to a simmer.
5. Stir in diced tomatoes.
6. Simmer for about 15-20 minutes, until eggplant is tender.
7. Use an immersion blender to blend the soup until smooth.
8. Season with salt and pepper.
9. Serve the eggplant tomato bisque hot.

Nutritional Information (per serving):
Cal: 190 | Carbs: 28g | Pro: 6g | Fat: 6g | Sugars: 11g | Fiber: 10g | Sodium: 900mg

16. Chicken Orzo Soup

Preparation time: 25 minutes
Servings: 2

Ingredients:

- 4 cups low-sodium chicken broth
- 1/2 cup diced cooked chicken breast
- 1/4 cup whole wheat orzo pasta
- 1 carrot, diced
- 1 celery stalk, diced
- 1/2 onion, diced
- 1 teaspoon olive oil
- Salt and pepper to taste

Instructions:

1. In a pot, heat olive oil over medium heat.
2. Add diced onion, carrot, and celery. Sauté until slightly softened.
3. Add diced cooked chicken and vegetable broth.
4. Simmer for about 10 minutes.
5. Stir in orzo pasta and cook until tender.
6. Season with salt and pepper.
7. Serve the chicken orzo soup hot.

Nutritional Information (per serving):
Cal: 220 | Carbs: 30g | Pro: 15g | Fat: 4g | Sugars: 5g | Fiber: 5g | Sodium: 900mg

17. Spinach Feta Chowder

Preparation time: 25 minutes
Servings: 2

Ingredients:

- 4 cups low-sodium vegetable broth
- 2 cups fresh spinach leaves
- 1/2 cup diced potatoes
- 1/2 cup diced onion
- 1/4 cup crumbled feta cheese
- 1 tablespoon olive oil
- Salt and pepper to taste

Instructions:

1. In a pot, heat olive oil over medium heat.
2. Add diced onion and diced potatoes. Sauté until slightly softened.
3. Add vegetable broth and bring to a simmer.
4. Stir in fresh spinach leaves and cook until wilted.
5. Season with salt and pepper.
6. Serve the spinach feta chowder hot, topped with crumbled feta.

Nutritional Information (per serving):
Cal: 220 | Carbs: 28g | Pro: 8g | Fat: 8g | Sugars: 4g | Fiber: 6g | Sodium: 800mg

18. Gazpacho Andaluz

Preparation time: 20 minutes
Servings: 2

Ingredients:

- 2 cups diced tomatoes
- 1/2 cucumber, peeled and diced
- 1/2 red bell pepper, diced
- 1/2 onion, diced
- 1 garlic clove, minced
- 2 tablespoons olive oil
- 2 tablespoons red wine vinegar
- Salt and pepper to taste

Instructions:

1. In a blender, combine diced tomatoes, cucumber, red bell pepper, diced onion, and minced garlic.
2. Blend until smooth.
3. Add olive oil and red wine vinegar. Blend again.
4. Season with salt and pepper.
5. Chill the gazpacho in the refrigerator for at least 1 hour before serving.
6. Serve the gazpacho Andaluz cold.

Nutritional Information (per serving):
Cal: 180 | Carbs: 16g | Pro: 2g | Fat: 12g | Sugars: 8g | Fiber: 4g | Sodium: 20mg

19. Artichoke Heart Soup

Preparation time: 25 minutes
Servings: 2

Ingredients:

- 2 cups low-sodium vegetable broth
- 1 can (14 oz) artichoke hearts, drained and chopped
- 1/2 onion, diced
- 1 garlic clove, minced
- 1 tablespoon olive oil
- 1/4 cup plain Greek yogurt
- Fresh parsley (for garnish)
- Salt and pepper to taste

Instructions:

1. In a pot, heat olive oil over medium heat.
2. Add diced onion and minced garlic. Cook until onion is translucent.
3. Add chopped artichoke hearts and vegetable broth.
4. Simmer for about 10 minutes.
5. Use an immersion blender to blend the soup until smooth.
6. Stir in plain Greek yogurt until well combined.
7. Season with salt and pepper.
8. Serve the artichoke heart soup warm, garnished with fresh parsley.

Nutritional Information (per serving):
Cal: 180 | Carbs: 20g | Pro: 6g | Fat: 9g | Sugars: 5g | Fiber: 7g | Sodium: 900mg

20. Pumpkin Walnut Bisque

Preparation time: 30 minutes
Servings: 2

Ingredients:

- 2 cups canned pumpkin puree
- 4 cups low-sodium vegetable broth
- 1/2 cup chopped walnuts
- 1/2 onion, diced
- 1 garlic clove, minced
- 1 tablespoon olive oil
- 1/2 teaspoon ground cinnamon
- Salt and pepper to taste

Instructions:

1. In a pot, heat olive oil over medium heat.
2. Add diced onion and minced garlic. Sauté until onion is translucent.
3. Add canned pumpkin puree and vegetable broth.
4. Simmer for about 10-15 minutes.
5. Stir in ground cinnamon and chopped walnuts.
6. Season with salt and pepper.
7. Serve the pumpkin walnut bisque hot.

Nutritional Information (per serving):
Cal: 230 | Carbs: 23g | Pro: 6g | Fat: 15g | Sugars: 7g | Fiber: 10g | Sodium: 800mg

Poultry

1. Lemon Herb Chicken

Preparation time: 10 minutes
Servings: 2

Ingredients:

- 2 boneless, skinless chicken breasts
- 2 tablespoons fresh lemon juice
- 1 tablespoon olive oil
- 2 cloves garlic, minced
- 1 teaspoon dried oregano
- Salt and pepper to taste

Instructions:

1. In a bowl, mix together lemon juice, olive oil, minced garlic, and dried oregano.
2. Season chicken breasts with salt and pepper.
3. Pour the lemon herb marinade over the chicken and let it marinate for at least 30 minutes.
4. Preheat a grill or grill pan over medium-high heat.
5. Grill the chicken for about 6-8 minutes per side, until cooked through.
6. Serve the lemon herb chicken with your choice of Mediterranean side dishes.

Nutritional Information (per serving):
Cal: 200 | Carbs: 2g | Pro: 28g | Fat: 9g | Sugars: 0g | Fiber: 0g | Sodium: 150mg

2. Greek Yogurt Marinade

Preparation time: 10 minutes
Servings: 2

Ingredients:

- 2 boneless, skinless chicken breasts
- 1/2 cup plain Greek yogurt
- 2 tablespoons fresh lemon juice
- 2 cloves garlic, minced
- 1 teaspoon dried oregano
- Salt and pepper to taste

Instructions:

1. In a bowl, mix together Greek yogurt, lemon juice, minced garlic, and dried oregano.
2. Season chicken breasts with salt and pepper.
3. Coat the chicken with the Greek yogurt marinade and let it marinate for at least 30 minutes.
4. Preheat a grill or grill pan over medium-high heat.
5. Grill the chicken for about 6-8 minutes per side, until cooked through.
6. Serve the Greek yogurt marinated chicken with Mediterranean-inspired sides.

Nutritional Information (per serving):

Cal: 220 | Carbs: 3g | Pro: 30g | Fat: 9g | Sugars: 1g | Fiber: 0g | Sodium: 200mg

3. Mediterranean Stuffed Turkey

Preparation time: 20 minutes
Cook time: 40 minutes
Servings: 2

Ingredients:

- 2 turkey breasts, boneless and skinless
- 1/2 cup chopped spinach
- 1/4 cup crumbled feta cheese
- 1/4 cup sun-dried tomatoes, chopped
- 2 cloves garlic, minced
- 1 tablespoon olive oil
- Salt and pepper to taste

Instructions:

1. Preheat the oven to 375°F (190°C).
2. In a bowl, mix together chopped spinach, crumbled feta cheese, chopped sun-dried tomatoes, minced garlic, olive oil, salt, and pepper.
3. Create a pocket in each turkey breast by making a horizontal slit.
4. Stuff the spinach and feta mixture into the pockets.
5. Season the outside of the turkey breasts with additional salt and pepper.
6. Heat an oven-safe skillet over medium-high heat.
7. Sear the turkey breasts for about 2-3 minutes on each side.
8. Transfer the skillet to the preheated oven and roast for about 25-30 minutes, or until the turkey is cooked through.
9. Serve the Mediterranean stuffed turkey with your favorite Mediterranean sides.

Nutritional Information (per serving):
Cal: 280 | Carbs: 8g | Pro: 50g | Fat: 6g | Sugars: 3g | Fiber: 2g | Sodium: 450mg

4. Balsamic Glazed Quail

Preparation time: 15 minutes
Cook time: 15 minutes
Servings: 2

Ingredients:

- 4 quail, cleaned and halved
- 1/4 cup balsamic vinegar
- 2 tablespoons olive oil
- 1 tablespoon honey
- 2 cloves garlic, minced
- Salt and pepper to taste

Instructions:

1. In a bowl, whisk together balsamic vinegar, olive oil, honey, minced garlic, salt, and pepper.
2. Place quail halves in a shallow dish and pour the balsamic glaze over them. Marinate for about 30 minutes.
3. Preheat a grill or grill pan over medium-high heat.
4. Grill the quail halves for about 5-7 minutes per side, brushing with the remaining balsamic glaze while cooking.
5. Serve the balsamic glazed quail with Mediterranean-style sides.

Nutritional Information (per serving):
Cal: 240 | Carbs: 11g | Pro: 23g | Fat: 12g | Sugars: 9g | Fiber: 0g | Sodium: 150mg

5. Rosemary Roast Chicken

Preparation time: 10 minutes
Cook time: 40 minutes
Servings: 2

Ingredients:

- 2 bone-in, skin-on chicken thighs
- 1 tablespoon olive oil
- 2 teaspoons fresh rosemary, chopped
- 2 cloves garlic, minced
- Salt and pepper to taste

Instructions:

1. Preheat the oven to 400°F (200°C).
2. In a bowl, mix together olive oil, chopped rosemary, minced garlic, salt, and pepper.
3. Rub the rosemary mixture all over the chicken thighs, including under the skin.
4. Place the chicken thighs on a baking sheet lined with parchment paper.
5. Roast in the preheated oven for about 35-40 minutes, until the chicken is cooked through and skin is crispy.
6. Serve the rosemary roast chicken with Mediterranean sides.

Nutritional Information (per serving):
Cal: 320 | Carbs: 0g | Pro: 26g | Fat: 24g | Sugars: 0g | Fiber: 0g | Sodium: 300mg

6. Olive Oil Grilled Turkey

Preparation time: 10 minutes
Cook time: 15 minutes
Servings: 2

Ingredients:

- 2 turkey tenderloins
- 2 tablespoons olive oil
- 1 teaspoon dried thyme
- 1 teaspoon dried oregano
- Salt and pepper to taste

Instructions:

1. Preheat a grill or grill pan over medium-high heat.
2. In a bowl, mix together olive oil, dried thyme, dried oregano, salt, and pepper.
3. Brush the turkey tenderloins with the olive oil mixture.
4. Grill the turkey tenderloins for about 6-8 minutes per side, until cooked through.
5. Let the turkey rest for a few minutes before slicing.
6. Serve the olive oil grilled turkey with Mediterranean-style accompaniments.

Nutritional Information (per serving):
Cal: 220 | Carbs: 1g | Pro: 32g | Fat: 10g | Sugars: 0g | Fiber: 0g | Sodium: 100mg

7. Herbed Chicken Skewers

Preparation time: 15 minutes
Cook time: 10 minutes
Servings: 2

Ingredients:

- 2 boneless, skinless chicken breasts, cut into cubes
- 2 tablespoons olive oil
- 1 tablespoon fresh lemon juice
- 1 teaspoon dried oregano
- 1 teaspoon dried thyme
- Salt and pepper to taste

Instructions:

1. In a bowl, whisk together olive oil, lemon juice, dried oregano, dried thyme, salt, and pepper.
2. Thread the chicken cubes onto skewers.
3. Brush the chicken skewers with the herbed marinade.
4. Preheat a grill or grill pan over medium-high heat.
5. Grill the chicken skewers for about 4-5 minutes per side, until cooked through.
6. Serve the herbed chicken skewers with Mediterranean sides.

Nutritional Information (per serving):
Cal: 240 | Carbs: 2g | Pro: 32g | Fat: 11g | Sugars: 1g | Fiber: 0g | Sodium: 150mg

8. Citrus Marinated Duck

Preparation time: 10 minutes
Cook time: 25 minutes
Servings: 2

Ingredients:

- 2 duck breasts
- 2 tablespoons orange juice
- 1 tablespoon lemon juice
- 1 tablespoon olive oil
- 1 teaspoon dried thyme
- Salt and pepper to taste

Instructions:

1. In a bowl, whisk together orange juice, lemon juice, olive oil, dried thyme, salt, and pepper.
2. Score the skin of the duck breasts.
3. Place the duck breasts in a shallow dish and pour the citrus marinade over them. Marinate for about 20 minutes.
4. Preheat a skillet over medium-high heat.
5. Place the duck breasts in the skillet, skin side down, and cook for about 4-5 minutes until the skin is crispy.
6. Flip the duck breasts and cook for another 3-4 minutes for medium doneness.
7. Let the duck breasts rest for a few minutes before slicing.
8. Serve the citrus marinated duck with your favorite Mediterranean sides.

Nutritional Information (per serving):
Cal: 350 | Carbs: 2g | Pro: 21g | Fat: 29g | Sugars: 1g | Fiber: 0g | Sodium: 80mg

9. Garlic Roasted Cornish Hens

Preparation time: 15 minutes
Cook time: 45 minutes
Servings: 2

Ingredients:

- 2 Cornish hens
- 4 cloves garlic, minced
- 2 tablespoons olive oil
- 1 teaspoon dried rosemary
- Salt and pepper to taste

Instructions:

1. Preheat the oven to 375°F (190°C).
2. In a bowl, mix together minced garlic, olive oil, dried rosemary, salt, and pepper.
3. Rub the garlic and rosemary mixture over the Cornish hens, both inside and out.
4. Place the Cornish hens on a baking sheet.
5. Roast in the preheated oven for about 40-45 minutes, until the hens are cooked through and golden brown.
6. Let the Cornish hens rest for a few minutes before serving.
7. Serve the garlic roasted Cornish hens with Medi-

-terranean-style accompaniments.

Nutritional Information (per serving):
Cal: 350 | Carbs: 0g | Pro: 30g | Fat: 25g | Sugars: 0g | Fiber: 0g | Sodium: 120mg

10. Yogurt Mint Chicken

Preparation time: 15 minutes
Cook time: 20 minutes
Servings: 2

Ingredients:

- 2 boneless, skinless chicken breasts
- 1/2 cup plain Greek yogurt
- 2 tablespoons fresh mint, chopped
- 1 tablespoon olive oil
- 1 teaspoon lemon zest
- Salt and pepper to taste

Instructions:

1. In a bowl, mix together Greek yogurt, chopped mint, olive oil, lemon zest, salt, and pepper.
2. Season chicken breasts with salt and pepper.
3. Coat the chicken with the yogurt mint mixture and let it marinate for at least 30 minutes.
4. Preheat a skillet over medium-high heat.
5. Cook the chicken breasts for about 8-10 minutes per side, until cooked through.
6. Serve the yogurt mint chicken with Mediterranean-inspired sides.

Nutritional Information (per serving):
Cal: 250 | Carbs: 4g | Pro: 30g | Fat: 11g | Sugars: 2g | Fiber: 0g | Sodium: 150mg

11. Tomato Basil Turkey

Preparation time: 10 minutes
Cook time: 25 minutes
Servings: 2

Ingredients:

- 2 turkey cutlets
- 1 cup cherry tomatoes, halved
- 1/4 cup fresh basil leaves, chopped
- 2 cloves garlic, minced
- 2 tablespoons olive oil
- Salt and pepper to taste

Instructions:

1. In a bowl, mix together cherry tomatoes, chopped basil, minced garlic, olive oil, salt, and pepper.
2. Season turkey cutlets with salt and pepper.

3. Heat a skillet over medium-high heat.
4. Cook the turkey cutlets for about 3-4 minutes per side, until cooked through.
5. Top the cooked turkey with the tomato basil mixture.
6. Serve the tomato basil turkey with Mediterranean sides.

Nutritional Information (per serving):
Cal: 280 | Carbs: 6g | Pro: 30g | Fat: 16g | Sugars: 3g | Fiber: 2g | Sodium: 150mg

12. Almond Crusted Chicken

Preparation time: 15 minutes
Cook time: 20 minutes
Servings: 2

Ingredients:

- 2 boneless, skinless chicken breasts
- 1/2 cup almond flour
- 2 tablespoons grated Parmesan cheese
- 1 teaspoon dried thyme
- 1 teaspoon lemon zest
- 1 egg, beaten
- Salt and pepper to taste

Instructions:

1. Preheat the oven to 400°F (200°C).
2. In a shallow bowl, mix together almond flour, grated Parmesan cheese, dried thyme, lemon zest, salt, and pepper.
3. Dip each chicken breast in the beaten egg, then coat it with the almond flour mixture.
4. Place the coated chicken breasts on a baking sheet.
5. Bake in the preheated oven for about 15-20 minutes, until the chicken is cooked through and almond crust is golden.
6. Serve the almond crusted chicken with your favorite Mediterranean sides.

Nutritional Information (per serving):
Cal: 320 | Carbs: 6g | Pro: 30g | Fat: 20g | Sugars: 1g | Fiber: 3g | Sodium: 300mg

13. Lemon Thyme Turkey

Preparation time: 10 minutes
Cook time: 25 minutes
Servings: 2

Ingredients:

- 2 turkey cutlets
- 2 tablespoons fresh lemon juice
- 1 tablespoon fresh thyme leaves
- 2 cloves garlic, minced
- 2 tablespoons olive oil
- Salt and pepper to taste

Instructions:

1. In a bowl, mix together fresh lemon juice, thyme leaves, minced garlic, olive oil, salt, and pepper.
2. Season turkey cutlets with salt and pepper.
3. Heat a skillet over medium-high heat.
4. Cook the turkey cutlets for about 3-4 minutes per side, until cooked through.
5. Drizzle the lemon thyme mixture over the cooked turkey.
6. Serve the lemon thyme turkey with Mediterranean-style accompaniments.

Nutritional Information (per serving):
Cal: 260 | Carbs: 2g | Pro: 30g | Fat: 14g | Sugars: 0g | Fiber: 0g | Sodium: 150mg

14. Greek Lemon Chicken

Preparation time: 10 minutes
Cook time: 30 minutes
Servings: 2

Ingredients:

- 2 chicken thighs, bone-in and skin-on
- 1/4 cup fresh lemon juice
- 2 tablespoons olive oil
- 1 teaspoon dried oregano
- 2 cloves garlic, minced
- Salt and pepper to taste

Instructions:

1. In a bowl, mix together fresh lemon juice, olive oil, dried oregano, minced garlic, salt, and pepper.
2. Season chicken thighs with salt and pepper.
3. Place the chicken thighs in a resealable plastic bag and pour the lemon marinade over them. Marinate for about 20 minutes.
4. Preheat the oven to 375°F (190°C).
5. Transfer the chicken thighs to a baking dish and pour the marinade over them.
6. Roast in the preheated oven for about 25-30 minutes, until the chicken is cooked through and the skin is crispy.
7. Serve the Greek lemon chicken with Mediterranean sides.

Nutritional Information (per serving):
Cal: 350 | Carbs: 3g | Pro: 25g | Fat: 26g | Sugars: 1g | Fiber: 0g | Sodium: 150mg

15. Mediterranean Pesto Chicken

Preparation time: 15 minutes
Cook time: 20 minutes

Servings: 2

Ingredients:

- 2 boneless, skinless chicken breasts
- 1/4 cup fresh basil leaves
- 2 tablespoons pine nuts
- 2 cloves garlic, minced
- 2 tablespoons grated Parmesan cheese
- 2 tablespoons olive oil
- Salt and pepper to taste

Instructions:

1. In a food processor, combine fresh basil leaves, pine nuts, minced garlic, grated Parmesan cheese, olive oil, salt, and pepper. Blend until you get a pesto sauce.
2. Season chicken breasts with salt and pepper.
3. Preheat a skillet over medium-high heat.
4. Cook the chicken breasts for about 5-6 minutes per side, until cooked through.
5. Top each chicken breast with a spoonful of Mediterranean pesto sauce.
6. Serve the Mediterranean pesto chicken with your favorite sides.

Nutritional Information (per serving):
Cal: 310 | Carbs: 3g | Pro: 30g | Fat: 20g | Sugars: 0g | Fiber: 1g | Sodium: 300mg

16. Feta Stuffed Chicken

Preparation time: 15 minutes
Cook time: 25 minutes
Servings: 2

Ingredients:

- 2 boneless, skinless chicken breasts
- 1/4 cup crumbled feta cheese
- 2 tablespoons chopped fresh spinach
- 2 cloves garlic, minced
- 1 tablespoon olive oil
- Salt and pepper to taste

Instructions:

1. Preheat the oven to 375°F (190°C).
2. In a bowl, mix together crumbled feta cheese, chopped fresh spinach, minced garlic, olive oil, salt, and pepper.
3. Make a pocket in each chicken breast by cutting a horizontal slit.
4. Stuff the feta and spinach mixture into the pockets.
5. Season the outside of the chicken breasts with additional salt and pepper.
6. Heat an oven-safe skillet over medium-high heat.
7. Sear the chicken breasts for about 2-3 minutes per side.

8. Transfer the skillet to the preheated oven and roast for about 15-20 minutes, or until the chicken is cooked through.
9. Serve the feta stuffed chicken with Mediterranean-style accompaniments.

Nutritional Information (per serving):
Cal: 250 | Carbs: 2g | Pro: 30g | Fat: 12g | Sugars: 0g | Fiber: 1g | Sodium: 300mg

17. Olive Rosemary Roast Hen

Preparation time: 15 minutes
Cook time: 1 hour 15 minutes
Servings: 2

Ingredients:

- 1 Cornish hen
- 1/4 cup pitted Kalamata olives, chopped
- 1 tablespoon fresh rosemary, chopped
- 2 cloves garlic, minced
- 2 tablespoons olive oil
- Salt and pepper to taste

Instructions:

1. Preheat the oven to 375°F (190°C).
2. In a bowl, mix together chopped Kalamata olives, chopped rosemary, minced garlic, olive oil, salt, and pepper.
3. Rinse and pat dry the Cornish hen.
4. Gently separate the skin from the meat of the hen without fully removing it.
5. Spread the olive and rosemary mixture under the skin and over the meat.
6. Rub the skin of the hen with a little olive oil and season with salt and pepper.
7. Place the Cornish hen on a baking sheet.
8. Roast in the preheated oven for about 1 hour and 15 minutes, or until the hen is cooked through and the skin is crispy.
9. Let the Cornish hen rest for a few minutes before serving.
10. Serve the olive rosemary roast hen with Mediterranean sides.

Nutritional Information (per serving):
Cal: 350 | Carbs: 2g | Pro: 25g | Fat: 26g | Sugars: 0g | Fiber: 1g | Sodium: 200mg

18. Herb Grilled Quail

Preparation time: 10 minutes
Cook time: 15 minutes
Servings: 2

Ingredients:

- 4 quail, cleaned and halved

- 2 tablespoons chopped fresh herbs (such as rosemary, thyme, and oregano)
- 2 cloves garlic, minced
- 2 tablespoons olive oil
- Salt and pepper to taste

Instructions:

1. In a bowl, mix together chopped fresh herbs, minced garlic, olive oil, salt, and pepper.
2. Place quail halves in a shallow dish and pour the herb mixture over them. Marinate for about 30 minutes.
3. Preheat a grill or grill pan over medium-high heat.
4. Grill the quail halves for about 5-7 minutes per side, until cooked through.
5. Serve the herb-grilled quail with Mediterranean-style accompaniments.

Nutritional Information (per serving):
Cal: 280 | Carbs: 0g | Pro: 30g | Fat: 18g | Sugars: 0g | Fiber: 0g | Sodium: 150mg

19. Orange Glazed Turkey

Preparation time: 10 minutes
Cook time: 25 minutes
Servings: 2

Ingredients:

- 2 turkey cutlets
- 1/4 cup fresh orange juice
- 2 tablespoons olive oil
- 2 tablespoons honey
- 1 teaspoon grated orange zest
- Salt and pepper to taste

Instructions:

1. In a bowl, mix together fresh orange juice, olive oil, honey, grated orange zest, salt, and pepper.
2. Season turkey cutlets with salt and pepper.
3. Heat a skillet over medium-high heat.
4. Cook the turkey cutlets for about 3-4 minutes per side, until cooked through.
5. Pour the orange glaze over the cooked turkey.
6. Serve the orange glazed turkey with Mediterranean sides.

Nutritional Information (per serving):
Cal: 280 | Carbs: 13g | Pro: 30g | Fat: 12g | Sugars: 12g | Fiber: 0g | Sodium: 150mg

20. Greek Souvlaki Chicken

Preparation time: 15 minutes
Cook time: 15 minutes
Servings: 2

Ingredients:

- 2 boneless, skinless chicken breasts, cut into cubes
- 2 tablespoons fresh lemon juice
- 2 tablespoons olive oil
- 2 cloves garlic, minced
- 1 teaspoon dried oregano
- Salt and pepper to taste

Instructions:

1. In a bowl, mix together fresh lemon juice, olive oil, minced garlic, dried oregano, salt, and pepper.
2. Season chicken cubes with salt and pepper.
3. Thread the chicken cubes onto skewers.
4. Preheat a grill or grill pan over medium-high heat.
5. Grill the chicken skewers for about 3-4 minutes per side, until cooked through.
6. Serve the Greek souvlaki chicken with Mediterranean sides.

Nutritional Information (per serving):
Cal: 240 | Carbs: 2g | Pro: 30g | Fat: 12g | Sugars: 0g | Fiber: 0g | Sodium: 150mg

Beef and Pork

1. Herb Grilled Steak

Preparation time: 10 minutes
Cook time: 10 minutes
Servings: 2

Ingredients:

- 2 beef sirloin steaks (6 oz each)
- 2 tablespoons fresh rosemary, chopped
- 2 tablespoons fresh thyme, chopped
- 2 cloves garlic, minced
- 2 tablespoons olive oil
- Salt and pepper to taste

Instructions:

1. Preheat a grill or grill pan over medium-high heat.
2. In a bowl, mix together chopped rosemary, chopped thyme, minced garlic, olive oil, salt, and pepper.
3. Rub the herb mixture onto both sides of the steaks.
4. Grill the steaks for about 4-5 minutes per side for medium-rare, or adjust cooking time to your preference.
5. Let the steaks rest for a few minutes before slicing.
6. Serve the herb-grilled steak with Mediterranean-style sides.

Nutritional Information (per serving):
Cal: 320 | Carbs: 1g | Pro: 40g | Fat: 18g | Sugars: 0g | Fiber: 0g | Sodium: 80mg

2. Mediterranean Beef Skewers

Preparation time: 15 minutes
Cook time: 10 minutes
Servings: 2

Ingredients:

- 8 oz beef tenderloin, cut into cubes
- 1/4 cup red onion, chopped
- 1/4 cup bell pepper, chopped
- 2 tablespoons olive oil
- 1 tablespoon fresh lemon juice
- 1 teaspoon dried oregano
- Salt and pepper to taste

Instructions:

1. Preheat a grill or grill pan over medium-high heat.
2. In a bowl, mix together olive oil, lemon juice, dried oregano, salt, and pepper.
3. Thread the beef cubes onto skewers, alternating with chopped red onion and bell pepper.
4. Brush the beef skewers with the olive oil mixture.
5. Grill the skewers for about 2-3 minutes per side, until the beef is cooked to your desired doneness.
6. Serve the Mediterranean beef skewers with your favorite sides.

Nutritional Information (per serving):
Cal: 280 | Carbs: 4g | Pro: 22g | Fat: 20g | Sugars: 1g | Fiber: 1g | Sodium: 80mg

3. Pork Tenderloin Citrus

Preparation time: 10 minutes
Cook time: 20 minutes
Servings: 2

Ingredients:

- 1 pork tenderloin (12 oz)
- 1/4 cup fresh orange juice
- 2 tablespoons olive oil
- 1 teaspoon dried thyme
- 2 cloves garlic, minced
- Salt and pepper to taste

Instructions:

1. Preheat the oven to 400°F (200°C).
2. In a bowl, mix together fresh orange juice, olive oil, dried thyme, minced garlic, salt, and pepper.
3. Season the pork tenderloin with salt and pepper.
4. Heat an oven-safe skillet over medium-high heat.
5. Sear the pork tenderloin for about 2-3 minutes per side.
6. Brush the tenderloin with the orange juice mixture.
7. Transfer the skillet to the preheated oven and roast for about 15-18 minutes, until the pork is cooked through.
8. Let the pork rest for a few minutes before slicing.
9. Serve the citrus-infused pork tenderloin with Mediterranean sides.

Nutritional Information (per serving):
Cal: 320 | Carbs: 6g | Pro: 30g | Fat: 18g | Sugars: 3g | Fiber: 1g | Sodium: 80mg

4. Greek Lamb Meatballs

Preparation time: 15 minutes
Cook time: 15 minutes
Servings: 2

Ingredients:

- 8 oz ground lamb
- 1/4 cup breadcrumbs
- 1/4 cup red onion, finely chopped
- 2 tablespoons fresh parsley, chopped
- 1 teaspoon dried oregano
- 1 egg
- Salt and pepper to taste

Instructions:

1. Preheat the oven to 375°F (190°C).
2. In a bowl, mix together ground lamb, breadcrumbs, chopped red onion, chopped parsley, dried oregano, beaten egg, salt, and pepper.
3. Shape the mixture into small meatballs.
4. Place the meatballs on a baking sheet lined with parchment paper.
5. Bake in the preheated oven for about 12-15 minutes, until the meatballs are cooked through.
6. Serve the Greek lamb meatballs with Mediterranean-style accompaniments.

Nutritional Information (per serving):
Cal: 320 | Carbs: 12g | Pro: 18g | Fat: 22g | Sugars: 2g | Fiber: 1g | Sodium: 300mg

5. Balsamic Glazed Pork

Preparation time: 10 minutes
Cook time: 20 minutes
Servings: 2

Ingredients:

- 2 pork chops (6 oz each)
- 2 tablespoons balsamic vinegar
- 1 tablespoon olive oil
- 1 tablespoon honey
- 1 teaspoon dried rosemary
- Salt and pepper to taste

Instructions:

1. In a bowl, mix together balsamic vinegar, olive oil, honey, dried rosemary, salt, and pepper.
2. Season pork chops with salt and pepper.
3. Heat a skillet over medium-high heat.
4. Cook the pork chops for about 4-5 minutes per side, until cooked through.
5. Pour the balsamic glaze over the cooked pork chops.
6. Serve the balsamic glazed pork with Mediterranean sides.

Nutritional Information (per serving):
Cal: 280 | Carbs: 8g | Pro: 30g | Fat: 12g | Sugars: 7g | Fiber: 0g | Sodium: 80mg

6. Rosemary Beef Stir Fry

Preparation time: 15 minutes
Cook time: 10 minutes
Servings: 2

Ingredients:

- 8 oz beef sirloin, thinly sliced
- 1 cup mixed bell peppers, sliced
- 1 cup zucchini, sliced
- 2 tablespoons olive oil
- 1 tablespoon fresh rosemary, chopped
- 2 cloves garlic, minced
- Salt and pepper to taste

Instructions:

1. Heat a skillet or wok over high heat.
2. Add olive oil and minced garlic, sauté for a few seconds.
3. Add sliced beef and stir-fry for about 2-3 minutes, until browned.
4. Add sliced bell peppers and zucchini, stir-fry for an additional 2-3 minutes.
5. Sprinkle chopped rosemary over the stir-fry, season with salt and pepper.
6. Stir-fry for another 1-2 minutes.
7. Serve the rosemary beef stir-fry with Mediterranean-inspired sides.

Nutritional Information (per serving):
Cal: 320 | Carbs: 10g | Pro: 24g | Fat: 20g | Sugars: 6g | Fiber: 3g | Sodium: 80mg

7. Lemon Garlic Pork Chops

Preparation time: 10 minutes
Cook time: 15 minutes
Servings: 2

Ingredients:

- 2 pork chops (6 oz each)
- 2 tablespoons fresh lemon juice
- 2 tablespoons olive oil
- 2 cloves garlic, minced
- 1 teaspoon dried oregano
- Salt and pepper to taste

Instructions:

1. In a bowl, mix together fresh lemon juice, olive oil, minced garlic, dried oregano, salt, and pepper.
2. Season pork chops with salt and pepper.
3. Heat a skillet over medium-high heat.
4. Cook the pork chops for about 4-5 minutes per side, until cooked through.
5. Pour the lemon garlic mixture over the cooked pork chops.
6. Serve the lemon garlic pork chops with Mediterranean sides.

Nutritional Information (per serving):
Cal: 280 | Carbs: 2g | Pro: 30g | Fat: 18g | Sugars: 0g | Fiber: 0g | Sodium: 80mg

8. Olive Crusted Beef

Preparation time: 15 minutes
Cook time: 15 minutes
Servings: 2

Ingredients:

- 2 beef tenderloin steaks (6 oz each)
- 1/4 cup Kalamata olives, chopped
- 2 tablespoons grated Parmesan cheese
- 2 tablespoons fresh parsley, chopped
- 2 tablespoons olive oil
- Salt and pepper to taste

Instructions:

1. Preheat a skillet over medium-high heat.
2. In a bowl, mix together chopped olives, grated Parmesan cheese, chopped parsley, olive oil, salt, and pepper.
3. Press the olive mixture onto both sides of the steaks.
4. Cook the steaks for about 4-5 minutes per side for medium-rare, or adjust cooking time to your preference.
5. Let the steaks rest for a few minutes before slicing.
6. Serve the olive crusted beef with Mediterranean-style sides.

Nutritional Information (per serving):
Cal: 340 | Carbs: 2g | Pro: 40g | Fat: 20g | Sugars: 0g | Fiber: 0g | Sodium: 200mg

9. Feta Stuffed Pork

Preparation time: 15 minutes
Cook time: 25 minutes
Servings: 2

Ingredients:

- 2 pork loin chops (6 oz each)
- 1/4 cup crumbled feta cheese
- 2 tablespoons chopped fresh spinach
- 2 cloves garlic, minced
- 1 tablespoon olive oil
- Salt and pepper to taste

Instructions:

1. Preheat the oven to 375°F (190°C).
2. In a bowl, mix together crumbled feta cheese, chopped spinach, minced garlic, olive oil, salt, and pepper.
3. Make a pocket in each pork chop by cutting a horizontal slit.
4. Stuff the feta and spinach mixture into the pockets.
5. Season the outside of the pork chops with additio-

nal salt and pepper.
6. Heat an oven-safe skillet over medium-high heat.
7. Sear the pork chops for about 2-3 minutes per side.
8. Transfer the skillet to the preheated oven and roast for about 15-20 minutes, until the pork is cooked through.
9. Let the pork chops rest for a few minutes before serving.
10. Serve the feta stuffed pork chops with Mediterranean sides.

Nutritional Information (per serving):
Cal: 340 | Carbs: 4g | Pro: 30g | Fat: 20g | Sugars: 1g | Fiber: 1g | Sodium: 400mg

10. Yogurt Marinated Lamb

Preparation time: 15 minutes (plus marinating time)
Cook time: 15 minutes
Servings: 2

Ingredients:

- 8 oz lamb leg steak, cut into cubes
- 1/2 cup plain Greek yogurt
- 2 tablespoons fresh mint, chopped
- 1 tablespoon olive oil
- 1 teaspoon ground cumin
- Salt and pepper to taste

Instructions:

1. In a bowl, mix together Greek yogurt, chopped mint, olive oil, ground cumin, salt, and pepper.
2. Season the lamb cubes with salt and pepper.
3. Coat the lamb with the yogurt mint mixture and let it marinate for at least 1 hour (or up to 4 hours) in the refrigerator.
4. Preheat a skillet over medium-high heat.
5. Thread the marinated lamb cubes onto skewers.
6. Grill the lamb skewers for about 2-3 minutes per side, until cooked through.
7. Serve the yogurt marinated lamb skewers with Mediterranean-style accompaniments.

Nutritional Information (per serving):
Cal: 320 | Carbs: 5g | Pro: 28g | Fat: 20g | Sugars: 2g | Fiber: 1g | Sodium: 100mg

11. Spinach Stuffed Beef

Preparation time: 20 minutes
Cook time: 25 minutes
Servings: 2

Ingredients:

- 2 beef sirloin steaks (6 oz each)
- 1 cup fresh spinach, chopped

- 1/4 cup crumbled feta cheese
- 2 cloves garlic, minced
- 2 tablespoons olive oil
- Salt and pepper to taste

Instructions:

1. Preheat the oven to 375°F (190°C).
2. In a bowl, mix together chopped spinach, crumbled feta cheese, minced garlic, olive oil, salt, and pepper.
3. Make a horizontal slit in each steak to create a pocket.
4. Stuff the spinach and feta mixture into the pockets.
5. Season the outside of the steaks with salt and pepper.
6. Heat an oven-safe skillet over medium-high heat.
7. Sear the steaks for about 2-3 minutes per side.
8. Transfer the skillet to the preheated oven and roast for about 15-20 minutes, until the beef is cooked to your preference.
9. Let the stuffed beef rest before slicing.
10. Serve the spinach stuffed beef with Mediterranean sides.

Nutritional Information (per serving):
Cal: 340 | Carbs: 3g | Pro: 40g | Fat: 18g | Sugars: 1g | Fiber: 1g | Sodium: 250mg

12. Mediterranean Pork Roast

Preparation time: 15 minutes
Cook time: 1 hour 15 minutes
Servings: 2

Ingredients:

- 1 pork loin roast (about 1 lb)
- 2 tablespoons olive oil
- 1 tablespoon dried oregano
- 2 cloves garlic, minced
- 1 lemon, sliced
- Salt and pepper to taste

Instructions:

1. Preheat the oven to 325°F (165°C).
2. In a bowl, mix together olive oil, dried oregano, minced garlic, salt, and pepper.
3. Rub the mixture over the surface of the pork loin.
4. Place the pork loin in a roasting pan and arrange lemon slices on top.
5. Roast in the preheated oven for about 1 hour and 15 minutes, or until the internal temperature reaches 145°F (63°C).
6. Let the pork roast rest for 10 minutes before slicing.
7. Serve the Mediterranean pork roast with roasted vegetables and salad.

Nutritional Information (per serving):
Cal: 360 | Carbs: 1g | Pro: 45g | Fat: 18g | Sugars: 0g | Fiber: 0g | Sodium: 150mg

13. Greek Style Burgers

Preparation time: 15 minutes
Cook time: 10 minutes
Servings: 2

Ingredients:

- 8 oz lean ground beef
- 1/4 cup crumbled feta cheese
- 2 tablespoons red onion, finely chopped
- 1 tablespoon fresh oregano, chopped
- Salt and pepper to taste
- Lettuce leaves for serving

Instructions:

1. In a bowl, mix together lean ground beef, crumbled feta cheese, chopped red onion, chopped oregano, salt, and pepper.
2. Divide the mixture into two and shape into burger patties.
3. Preheat a grill or grill pan over medium-high heat.
4. Grill the burger patties for about 4-5 minutes per side, or until cooked to your desired doneness.
5. Serve the Greek-style burgers on lettuce leaves, alongside Mediterranean sides.

Nutritional Information (per serving):
Cal: 320 | Carbs: 2g | Pro: 30g | Fat: 20g | Sugars: 0g | Fiber: 0g | Sodium: 300mg

14. Herbed Pork Medallions

Preparation time: 15 minutes
Cook time: 15 minutes
Servings: 2

Ingredients:

- 1 pork tenderloin (about 12 oz)
- 2 tablespoons fresh rosemary, chopped
- 2 tablespoons fresh thyme, chopped
- 2 cloves garlic, minced
- 2 tablespoons olive oil
- Salt and pepper to taste

Instructions:

1. Preheat the oven to 400°F (200°C).
2. In a bowl, mix together chopped rosemary, chopped thyme, minced garlic, olive oil, salt, and pepper.
3. Slice the pork tenderloin into medallions, about 1 inch thick.
4. Coat the pork medallions with the herb mixture.

5. Heat a skillet over medium-high heat.
6. Cook the pork medallions for about 2-3 minutes per side, until browned.
7. Transfer the skillet to the preheated oven and roast for an additional 8-10 minutes, or until the pork is cooked through.
8. Serve the herbed pork medallions with Mediterranean sides.

Nutritional Information (per serving):
Cal: 300 | Carbs: 2g | Pro: 35g | Fat: 16g | Sugars: 0g | Fiber: 1g | Sodium: 80mg

15. Tomato Basil Beef

Preparation time: 10 minutes
Cook time: 20 minutes
Servings: 2

Ingredients:

- 2 beef sirloin steaks (6 oz each)
- 1 cup cherry tomatoes, halved
- 1/4 cup fresh basil leaves, chopped
- 2 cloves garlic, minced
- 2 tablespoons olive oil
- Salt and pepper to taste

Instructions:

1. Preheat a skillet over medium-high heat.
2. In a bowl, mix together cherry tomatoes, chopped basil, minced garlic, olive oil, salt, and pepper.
3. Season the steaks with salt and pepper.
4. Cook the steaks for about 4-5 minutes per side for medium-rare, or to your preference.
5. Top the cooked steaks with the tomato basil mixture.
6. Serve the tomato basil beef with Mediterranean-style sides.

Nutritional Information (per serving):
Cal: 340 | Carbs: 4g | Pro: 40g | Fat: 18g | Sugars: 2g | Fiber: 1g | Sodium: 100mg

16. Orange Glazed Pork

Preparation time: 10 minutes
Cook time: 20 minutes
Servings: 2

Ingredients:

- 2 pork loin chops (6 oz each)
- 1/4 cup fresh orange juice
- 2 tablespoons olive oil
- 2 tablespoons honey
- 1 teaspoon grated orange zest
- Salt and pepper to taste

Instructions:

1. In a bowl, mix together fresh orange juice, olive oil, honey, grated orange zest, salt, and pepper.
2. Season the pork chops with salt and pepper.
3. Heat a skillet over medium-high heat.
4. Cook the pork chops for about 4-5 minutes per side, until cooked through.
5. Pour the orange glaze over the cooked pork chops.
6. Serve the orange glazed pork with Mediterranean sides.

Nutritional Information (per serving):
Cal: 280 | Carbs: 13g | Pro: 30g | Fat: 12g | Sugars: 12g | Fiber: 0g | Sodium: 150mg

17. Mediterranean Beef Stew

Preparation time: 15 minutes
Cook time: 2 hours
Servings: 2

Ingredients:

- 12 oz beef stew meat, cubed
- 1 onion, chopped
- 2 cloves garlic, minced
- 1 can (14 oz) diced tomatoes
- 1 cup beef broth
- 1 teaspoon dried oregano
- 1 teaspoon dried rosemary
- Salt and pepper to taste

Instructions:

1. In a pot, heat olive oil over medium heat.
2. Add chopped onion and minced garlic, sauté until softened.
3. Add beef cubes and brown on all sides.
4. Stir in diced tomatoes, beef broth, dried oregano, dried rosemary, salt, and pepper.
5. Bring the mixture to a boil, then reduce the heat to low, cover, and simmer for about 1.5 to 2 hours, or until the beef is tender.
6. Serve the Mediterranean beef stew with whole grain bread or couscous.

Nutritional Information (per serving):
Cal: 350 | Carbs: 15g | Pro: 30g | Fat: 18g | Sugars: 6g | Fiber: 4g | Sodium: 700mg

18. Greek Pork Souvlaki

Preparation time: 25 minutes (plus marinating time)
Cook time: 10 minutes
Servings: 2

Ingredients:

- 8 oz pork tenderloin, cut into cubes
- 1/4 cup plain Greek yogurt
- 2 tablespoons fresh lemon juice
- 1 tablespoon olive oil
- 2 cloves garlic, minced
- 1 teaspoon dried oregano
- Salt and pepper to taste

Instructions:

1. In a bowl, mix together Greek yogurt, fresh lemon juice, olive oil, minced garlic, dried oregano, salt, and pepper.
2. Season the pork cubes with salt and pepper.
3. Coat the pork with the yogurt mixture and let it marinate for at least 1 hour (or up to 4 hours) in the refrigerator.
4. Preheat a grill or grill pan over medium-high heat.
5. Thread the marinated pork cubes onto skewers.
6. Grill the pork souvlaki for about 2-3 minutes per side, until cooked through.
7. Serve the Greek pork souvlaki with Mediterranean accompaniments.

Nutritional Information (per serving):
Cal: 280 | Carbs: 6g | Pro: 28g | Fat: 16g | Sugars: 3g | Fiber: 1g | Sodium: 150mg

19. Lemon Thyme Steak

Preparation time: 10 minutes
Cook time: 15 minutes
Servings: 2

Ingredients:

- 2 beef sirloin steaks (6 oz each)
- 2 tablespoons fresh lemon juice
- 2 tablespoons olive oil
- 1 tablespoon fresh thyme leaves
- 2 cloves garlic, minced
- Salt and pepper to taste

Instructions:

1. Preheat a skillet over medium-high heat.
2. In a bowl, mix together fresh lemon juice, olive oil, fresh thyme leaves, minced garlic, salt, and pepper.
3. Season the steaks with salt and pepper.
4. Cook the steaks for about 4-5 minutes per side for medium-rare, or to your desired doneness.
5. Pour the lemon thyme mixture over the cooked steaks.
6. Serve the lemon thyme steak with Mediterranean-style sides.

Nutritional Information (per serving):
Cal: 320 | Carbs: 2g | Pro: 40g | Fat: 18g | Sugars: 0g | Fiber: 0g | Sodium: 80mg

20. Olive Braised Pork

Preparation time: 15 minutes
Cook time: 1 hour 30 minutes
Servings: 2

Ingredients:

- 1 pork shoulder roast (about 1 lb)
- 1/2 cup Kalamata olives, pitted
- 1/4 cup red onion, chopped
- 2 cloves garlic, minced
- 1 cup low-sodium chicken broth
- 2 tablespoons olive oil
- Salt and pepper to taste

Instructions:

1. Preheat the oven to 325°F (165°C).
2. In a pot, heat olive oil over medium heat.
3. Add chopped red onion and minced garlic, sauté until softened.
4. Add pork shoulder roast and brown on all sides.
5. Add pitted Kalamata olives and low-sodium chicken broth to the pot.
6. Bring the mixture to a simmer, then cover and transfer to the preheated oven.
7. Braise the pork in the oven for about 1.5 hours, or until the meat is tender and fully cooked.
8. Remove the pork from the oven and let it rest for a few minutes.
9. Shred the pork and serve it with the olive and onion mixture.

Nutritional Information (per serving):
Cal: 380 | Carbs: 5g | Pro: 30g | Fat: 26g | Sugars: 1g | Fiber: 1g | Sodium: 600mg

Side Dishes

1. Greek Salad

Preparation time: 10 minutes
Servings: 2

Ingredients:

- 2 cups mixed salad greens
- 1/2 cucumber, diced
- 1/2 cup cherry tomatoes, halved
- 1/4 red onion, thinly sliced
- 1/4 cup Kalamata olives, pitted
- 1/4 cup crumbled feta cheese
- 2 tablespoons extra virgin olive oil
- 1 tablespoon red wine vinegar
- Salt and pepper to taste

Instructions:

1. In a salad bowl, combine mixed salad greens, diced cucumber, cherry tomatoes, red onion, Kalamata olives, and crumbled feta cheese.
2. Drizzle extra virgin olive oil and red wine vinegar over the salad.
3. Season with salt and pepper to taste.
4. Toss the ingredients to combine.
5. Serve the Greek salad as a refreshing side.

Nutritional Information (per serving):
Cal: 180 | Carbs: 8g | Pro: 4g | Fat: 15g | Sugars: 3g | Fiber: 2g | Sodium: 330mg

2. Lemon Roasted Veggies

Preparation time: 10 minutes
Cook time: 25 minutes
Servings: 2

Ingredients:

- 2 cups mixed vegetables (e.g., zucchini, bell peppers, carrots), chopped
- 2 tablespoons extra virgin olive oil
- 2 cloves garlic, minced
- 1 tablespoon fresh lemon juice
- 1 teaspoon dried oregano
- Salt and pepper to taste

Instructions:

1. Preheat the oven to 400°F (200°C).
2. In a bowl, toss mixed vegetables with extra virgin olive oil, minced garlic, lemon juice, dried oregano, salt, and pepper.
3. Spread the vegetables on a baking sheet in a single layer.
4. Roast in the preheated oven for about 20-25 minutes, until the vegetables are tender and slightly browned.
5. Serve the lemon roasted veggies as a flavorful side dish.

Nutritional Information (per serving):
Cal: 130 | Carbs: 10g | Pro: 2g | Fat: 10g | Sugars: 4g | Fiber: 3g | Sodium: 160mg

3. Hummus Trio

Preparation time: 10 minutes
Servings: 2

Ingredients:

- 1/2 cup classic hummus
- 1/2 cup roasted red pepper hummus
- 1/2 cup spinach and artichoke hummus
- 2 tablespoons extra virgin olive oil
- Fresh vegetables (e.g., cucumber, carrot, bell pepper, celery) for dipping

Instructions:

1. Arrange the three types of hummus on a serving plate.
2. Drizzle extra virgin olive oil over the hummus.
3. Wash, peel, and cut fresh vegetables into sticks.
4. Serve the hummus trio with the fresh vegetable sticks for dipping.

Nutritional Information (per serving):
Cal: 240 | Carbs: 14g | Pro: 6g | Fat: 18g | Sugars: 2g | Fiber: 6g | Sodium: 520mg

4. Olive Tapenade

Preparation time: 10 minutes
Servings: 2

Ingredients:

- 1/2 cup Kalamata olives, pitted
- 2 tablespoons capers, drained
- 2 tablespoons fresh parsley, chopped
- 1 tablespoon extra virgin olive oil
- 1 teaspoon lemon juice
- 1 small garlic clove, minced
- Pepper to taste

Instructions:

1. In a food processor, combine Kalamata olives, capers, chopped parsley, extra virgin olive oil, lemon juice, minced garlic, and a dash of pepper.
2. Pulse the mixture until well combined but slightly chunky.
3. Taste and adjust seasoning if needed.
4. Serve the olive tapenade as a tangy side or spread.

Nutritional Information (per serving):

Cal: 70 | Carbs: 3g | Pro: 1g | Fat: 6g | Sugars: 0g | Fiber: 1g | Sodium: 560mg

5. Quinoa Tabbouleh

Preparation time: 15 minutes
Cook time: 15 minutes
Servings: 2

Ingredients:

- 1/2 cup quinoa, rinsed
- 1 cup fresh parsley, chopped
- 1/2 cup cherry tomatoes, diced
- 1/4 cup red onion, finely chopped
- 2 tablespoons fresh lemon juice
- 2 tablespoons extra virgin olive oil
- Salt and pepper to taste

Instructions:

1. In a small pot, bring 1 cup of water to a boil.
2. Add rinsed quinoa, reduce heat to low, cover, and simmer for about 12-15 minutes, or until quinoa is cooked and water is absorbed.
3. Fluff the cooked quinoa with a fork and let it cool.
4. In a bowl, combine chopped parsley, diced cherry tomatoes, finely chopped red onion, cooked quinoa, fresh lemon juice, extra virgin olive oil, salt, and pepper.
5. Toss the ingredients to combine.
6. Serve the quinoa tabbouleh as a nutritious side.

Nutritional Information (per serving):
Cal: 210 | Carbs: 26g | Pro: 5g | Fat: 9g | Sugars: 2g | Fiber: 4g | Sodium: 40mg

6. Feta Stuffed Peppers

Preparation time: 10 minutes
Cook time: 25 minutes
Servings: 2

Ingredients:

- 2 large bell peppers (red, yellow, or orange)
- 1/2 cup cooked quinoa
- 1/4 cup crumbled feta cheese
- 2 tablespoons chopped fresh parsley
- 1 tablespoon extra virgin olive oil
- Salt and pepper to taste

Instructions:

1. Preheat the oven to 375°F (190°C).
2. Cut the tops off the bell peppers and remove the seeds and membranes.
3. In a bowl, mix together cooked quinoa, crumbled feta cheese, chopped parsley, extra virgin olive oil, salt, and pepper.

4. Stuff the quinoa mixture into the bell peppers.
5. Place the stuffed peppers in a baking dish.
6. Bake in the preheated oven for about 20-25 minutes, until the peppers are tender.
7. Serve the feta stuffed peppers as a delightful side.

Nutritional Information (per serving):
Cal: 180 | Carbs: 22g | Pro: 5g | Fat: 8g | Sugars: 8g | Fiber: 4g | Sodium: 400mg

7. Garlic Spinach Saute

Preparation time: 5 minutes
Cook time: 5 minutes
Servings: 2

Ingredients:

- 4 cups fresh spinach leaves
- 2 cloves garlic, minced
- 1 tablespoon extra virgin olive oil
- 1 teaspoon lemon juice
- Salt and pepper to taste

Instructions:

1. In a large skillet, heat extra virgin olive oil over medium heat.
2. Add minced garlic and sauté for about 1 minute, until fragrant.
3. Add fresh spinach leaves to the skillet.
4. Cook the spinach, tossing frequently, for about 2-3 minutes, until wilted.
5. Drizzle lemon juice over the cooked spinach.
6. Season with salt and pepper to taste.
7. Serve the garlic spinach sauté as a nutritious side.

Nutritional Information (per serving):
Cal: 70 | Carbs: 3g | Pro: 2g | Fat: 5g | Sugars: 0g | Fiber: 2g | Sodium: 180mg

8. Tomato Cucumber Salad

Preparation time: 10 minutes
Servings: 2

Ingredients:

- 1 cup cherry tomatoes, halved
- 1/2 cucumber, diced
- 2 tablespoons red onion, finely chopped
- 2 tablespoons fresh basil, chopped
- 1 tablespoon extra virgin olive oil
- 1 tablespoon balsamic vinegar
- Salt and pepper to taste

Instructions:

1. In a salad bowl, combine cherry tomatoes, diced cucumber, finely chopped red onion, and chop-

-ped fresh basil.
2. Drizzle extra virgin olive oil and balsamic vinegar over the salad.
3. Season with salt and pepper to taste.
4. Toss the ingredients to combine.
5. Serve the tomato cucumber salad as a refreshing side.

Nutritional Information (per serving):
Cal: 60 | Carbs: 5g | Pro: 1g | Fat: 4g | Sugars: 2g | Fiber: 1g | Sodium: 15mg

9. Eggplant Caponata

Preparation time: 15 minutes
Cook time: 25 minutes
Servings: 2

Ingredients:

- 1 small eggplant, diced
- 1/2 cup cherry tomatoes, halved
- 1/4 cup red onion, finely chopped
- 2 tablespoons Kalamata olives, pitted and chopped
- 2 tablespoons capers, drained
- 2 tablespoons extra virgin olive oil
- 2 tablespoons red wine vinegar
- Salt and pepper to taste

Instructions:

1. Heat extra virgin olive oil in a skillet over medium heat.
2. Add diced eggplant and sauté for about 5 minutes, until softened.
3. Stir in cherry tomatoes, finely chopped red onion, Kalamata olives, and capers.
4. Continue to cook for another 5-7 minutes, until the tomatoes start to break down.
5. Drizzle red wine vinegar over the mixture.
6. Season with salt and pepper to taste.
7. Cook for an additional 2 minutes.
8. Serve the eggplant caponata warm or at room temperature.

Nutritional Information (per serving):
Cal: 130 | Carbs: 10g | Pro: 2g | Fat: 10g | Sugars: 5g | Fiber: 3g | Sodium: 450mg

10. Mediterranean Rice Pilaf

Preparation time: 10 minutes
Cook time: 25 minutes
Servings: 2

Ingredients:

- 1/2 cup long-grain brown rice
- 1 cup low-sodium chicken or vegetable broth

- 1/4 cup red bell pepper, diced
- 1/4 cup green bell pepper, diced
- 2 tablespoons red onion, finely chopped
- 1 tablespoon extra virgin olive oil
- 1 teaspoon dried oregano
- Salt and pepper to taste

Instructions:

1. Rinse the brown rice under cold water.
2. In a pot, heat extra virgin olive oil over medium heat.
3. Add diced red bell pepper, green bell pepper, and finely chopped red onion. Sauté for about 2-3 minutes, until slightly softened.
4. Add the rinsed brown rice to the pot and sauté for another 2 minutes.
5. Pour in low-sodium chicken or vegetable broth.
6. Season with dried oregano, salt, and pepper.
7. Bring the mixture to a boil, then reduce the heat to low, cover, and simmer for about 20-25 minutes, or until the rice is cooked and the liquid is absorbed.
8. Fluff the cooked rice with a fork and let it rest for a few minutes.
9. Serve the Mediterranean rice pilaf as a wholesome side.

Nutritional Information (per serving):
Cal: 210 | Carbs: 39g | Pro: 4g | Fat: 4g | Sugars: 2g | Fiber: 4g | Sodium: 150mg

11. Roasted Red Onions

Preparation time: 10 minutes
Cook time: 25 minutes
Servings: 2

Ingredients:

- 2 medium red onions, peeled and sliced into thick rings
- 2 tablespoons extra virgin olive oil
- 1 teaspoon dried thyme
- Salt and pepper to taste

Instructions:

1. Preheat the oven to 375°F (190°C).
2. Toss red onion rings with extra virgin olive oil, dried thyme, salt, and pepper in a bowl.
3. Spread the onion rings on a baking sheet in a single layer.
4. Roast in the preheated oven for about 20-25 minutes, until the onions are soft and slightly caramelized.
5. Serve the roasted red onions as a flavorful side.

Nutritional Information (per serving):
Cal: 120 | Carbs: 10g | Pro: 1g | Fat: 9g | Sugars: 4g | Fiber: 2g | Sodium: 5mg

12. Greek Yogurt Dip

Preparation time: 15 minutes
Servings: 2

Ingredients:

* 1/2 cup Greek yogurt
* 1 tablespoon fresh lemon juice
* 1 clove garlic, minced
* 1 tablespoon fresh dill, chopped
* Salt and pepper to taste

Instructions:

1. In a bowl, mix together Greek yogurt, fresh lemon juice, minced garlic, chopped dill, salt, and pepper.
2. Taste and adjust seasoning if needed.
3. Serve the Greek yogurt dip with vegetable sticks or whole grain pita.

Nutritional Information (per serving):
Cal: 40 | Carbs: 3g | Pro: 6g | Fat: 1g | Sugars: 2g | Fiber: 0g | Sodium: 25mg

13. Balsamic Grilled Asparagus

Preparation time: 10 minutes
Cook time: 10 minutes
Servings: 2

Ingredients:

* 1 bunch asparagus, trimmed
* 2 tablespoons balsamic vinegar
* 1 tablespoon extra virgin olive oil
* Salt and pepper to taste

Instructions:

1. Preheat a grill or grill pan over medium-high heat.
2. In a bowl, toss asparagus with balsamic vinegar, extra virgin olive oil, salt, and pepper.
3. Grill the asparagus for about 3-5 minutes per side, until tender and slightly charred.
4. Serve the balsamic grilled asparagus as a flavorful side.

Nutritional Information (per serving):
Cal: 50 | Carbs: 6g | Pro: 3g | Fat: 3g | Sugars: 4g | Fiber: 2g | Sodium: 5mg

14. Artichoke Hearts Saute

Preparation time: 5 minutes
Cook time: 10 minutes
Servings: 2

Ingredients:

* 1 can (14 oz) artichoke hearts, drained and quartered
* 2 tablespoons extra virgin olive oil
* 2 cloves garlic, minced
* 1 tablespoon fresh lemon juice
* 1 teaspoon dried Italian herbs
* Salt and pepper to taste

Instructions:

1. In a skillet, heat extra virgin olive oil over medium heat.
2. Add minced garlic and sauté for about 1 minute, until fragrant.
3. Add quartered artichoke hearts to the skillet.
4. Cook the artichoke hearts for about 5-7 minutes, until heated through and slightly browned.
5. Drizzle fresh lemon juice over the sautéed artichoke hearts.
6. Season with dried Italian herbs, salt, and pepper.
7. Serve the artichoke hearts sauté as a simple side.

Nutritional Information (per serving):
Cal: 120 | Carbs: 7g | Pro: 3g | Fat: 9g | Sugars: 1g | Fiber: 3g | Sodium: 480mg

15. Chickpea Cucumber Salad

Preparation time: 10 minutes
Servings: 2

Ingredients:

* 1 can (15 oz) chickpeas, drained and rinsed
* 1/2 cucumber, diced
* 1/4 red onion, finely chopped
* 2 tablespoons fresh parsley, chopped
* 2 tablespoons extra virgin olive oil
* 1 tablespoon red wine vinegar
* Salt and pepper to taste

Instructions:

1. In a bowl, combine chickpeas, diced cucumber, finely chopped red onion, and chopped fresh parsley.
2. Drizzle extra virgin olive oil and red wine vinegar over the salad.
3. Season with salt and pepper to taste.
4. Toss the ingredients to combine.
5. Serve the chickpea cucumber salad as a satisfying side.

Nutritional Information (per serving):
Cal: 250 | Carbs: 28g | Pro: 8g | Fat: 12g | Sugars: 5g | Fiber: 8g | Sodium: 340mg

16. Roasted Brussels Sprouts

Preparation time: 10 minutes
Cook time: 20 minutes
Servings: 2

Ingredients:

- 1/2 lb Brussels sprouts, trimmed and halved
- 2 tablespoons extra virgin olive oil
- 1 tablespoon balsamic vinegar
- Salt and pepper to taste

Instructions:

1. Preheat the oven to 400°F (200°C).
2. Toss halved Brussels sprouts with extra virgin olive oil, balsamic vinegar, salt, and pepper in a bowl.
3. Spread the Brussels sprouts on a baking sheet in a single layer.
4. Roast in the preheated oven for about 15-20 minutes, until the sprouts are tender and slightly caramelized.
5. Serve the roasted Brussels sprouts as a flavorful side.

Nutritional Information (per serving):
Cal: 120 | Carbs: 12g | Pro: 4g | Fat: 7g | Sugars: 3g | Fiber: 4g | Sodium: 40mg

17. Spinach Feta Stuffed Mushrooms

Preparation time: 10 minutes
Cook time: 20 minutes
Servings: 2

Ingredients:

- 8 large button mushrooms, stems removed
- 1 cup fresh spinach leaves, chopped
- 1/4 cup crumbled feta cheese
- 2 cloves garlic, minced
- 2 tablespoons extra virgin olive oil
- Salt and pepper to taste

Instructions:

1. Preheat the oven to 375°F (190°C).
2. In a skillet, heat extra virgin olive oil over medium heat.
3. Add minced garlic and chopped spinach. Sauté for about 2 minutes, until the spinach wilts.
4. Remove the skillet from heat and mix in crumbled feta cheese, salt, and pepper.
5. Stuff the mushroom caps with the spinach-feta mixture.
6. Place the stuffed mushrooms on a baking sheet.
7. Bake in the preheated oven for about 15-20 minutes, until the mushrooms are tender and the filling is heated through.

8. Serve the spinach feta stuffed mushrooms as a delicious side.

Nutritional Information (per serving):
Cal: 130 | Carbs: 5g | Pro: 5g | Fat: 11g | Sugars: 2g | Fiber: 2g | Sodium: 250mg

18. Caprese Skewers

Preparation time: 10 minutes
Servings: 2

Ingredients:

- 12 cherry tomatoes
- 12 small fresh mozzarella balls
- 12 fresh basil leaves
- 2 tablespoons balsamic glaze
- Salt and pepper to taste

Instructions:

1. Assemble the skewers by threading a cherry tomato, a small mozzarella ball, and a fresh basil leaf onto each skewer.
2. Arrange the skewers on a serving platter.
3. Drizzle balsamic glaze over the caprese skewers.
4. Season with salt and pepper to taste.
5. Serve the caprese skewers as a delightful side.

Nutritional Information (per serving):
Cal: 160 | Carbs: 4g | Pro: 9g | Fat: 11g | Sugars: 2g | Fiber: 0g | Sodium: 280mg

19. Zucchini Ribbon Salad

Preparation time: 10 minutes
Servings: 2

Ingredients:

- 1 large zucchini
- 1 tablespoon extra virgin olive oil
- 1 tablespoon fresh lemon juice
- 2 tablespoons shaved Parmesan cheese
- 1 tablespoon chopped fresh mint
- Salt and pepper to taste

Instructions:

1. Use a vegetable peeler to create thin ribbons from the zucchini.
2. In a bowl, toss zucchini ribbons with extra virgin olive oil, fresh lemon juice, shaved Parmesan cheese, chopped fresh mint, salt, and pepper.
3. Toss the ingredients to combine.
4. Serve the zucchini ribbon salad as a light and refreshing side.

Nutritional Information (per serving):
Cal: 100 | Carbs: 5g | Pro: 4g | Fat: 7g | Sugars: 2g |
Fiber: 2g | Sodium: 150mg

20. Roasted Garlic Cauliflower

Preparation time: 10 minutes
Cook time: 25 minutes
Servings: 2

Ingredients:

- 1/2 head cauliflower, cut into florets
- 2 tablespoons extra virgin olive oil
- 2 cloves garlic, minced
- 1/2 teaspoon dried thyme
- Salt and pepper to taste

Instructions:

1. Preheat the oven to 400°F (200°C).
2. Toss cauliflower florets with extra virgin olive oil, minced garlic, dried thyme, salt, and pepper in a bowl.
3. Spread the cauliflower on a baking sheet in a single layer.
4. Roast in the preheated oven for about 20-25 minutes, until the cauliflower is tender and slightly browned.
5. Serve the roasted garlic cauliflower as a flavorful side.

Nutritional Information (per serving):
Cal: 90 | Carbs: 7g | Pro: 2g | Fat: 7g | Sugars: 2g |
Fiber: 3g | Sodium: 40mg

Vegetables and Grains

1. Quinoa Stuffed Peppers

Preparation time: 15 minutes
Preparation time: 30 minutes
Servings: 2

Ingredients:

* 2 large bell peppers, halved and seeds removed
* 1/2 cup cooked quinoa
* 1/2 cup canned black beans, drained and rinsed
* 1/4 cup diced tomatoes
* 1/4 cup crumbled feta cheese
* 1 tablespoon chopped fresh parsley
* Salt and pepper to taste

Instructions:

1. Preheat the oven to 375°F (190°C).
2. In a bowl, mix cooked quinoa, black beans, diced tomatoes, crumbled feta cheese, chopped parsley, salt, and pepper.
3. Stuff the quinoa mixture into the halved bell peppers.
4. Place the stuffed peppers in a baking dish.
5. Bake in the preheated oven for about 25-30 minutes, until the peppers are tender.
6. Serve the quinoa stuffed peppers as a wholesome meal.

Nutritional Information (per serving):
Cal: 250 | Carbs: 36g | Pro: 11g | Fat: 7g | Sugars: 5g | Fiber: 9g | Sodium: 470mg

2. Greek Chickpea Salad

Preparation time: 10 minutes
Servings: 2

Ingredients:

* 1 can (15 oz) chickpeas, drained and rinsed
* 1/2 cucumber, diced
* 1/2 cup cherry tomatoes, halved
* 1/4 red onion, finely chopped
* 1/4 cup crumbled feta cheese
* 2 tablespoons extra virgin olive oil
* 2 tablespoons fresh lemon juice
* Salt and pepper to taste

Instructions:

1. In a bowl, combine chickpeas, diced cucumber, cherry tomatoes, finely chopped red onion, and crumbled feta cheese.
2. Drizzle extra virgin olive oil and fresh lemon juice over the salad.
3. Season with salt and pepper to taste.
4. Toss the ingredients to combine.
5. Serve the Greek chickpea salad as a refreshing

meal.

Nutritional Information (per serving):
Cal: 330 | Carbs: 35g | Pro: 11g | Fat: 18g | Sugars: 6g | Fiber: 9g | Sodium: 470mg

3. Spinach Mushroom Risotto

Preparation time: 10 minutes
Preparation time: 25 minutes
Servings: 2

Ingredients:

* 1 cup Arborio rice
* 2 cups low-sodium vegetable broth
* 1 cup fresh spinach leaves
* 1 cup sliced mushrooms
* 1/4 cup grated Parmesan cheese
* 2 tablespoons extra virgin olive oil
* Salt and pepper to taste

Instructions:

1. In a pot, bring vegetable broth to a simmer and keep it warm.
2. In another pot, heat extra virgin olive oil over medium heat.
3. Add Arborio rice and sauté for about 2 minutes, until slightly translucent.
4. Gradually add warm vegetable broth, 1/2 cup at a time, stirring frequently and allowing the liquid to be absorbed before adding more.
5. When the rice is nearly cooked, stir in fresh spinach leaves and sliced mushrooms.
6. Continue adding broth and stirring until the rice is creamy and tender.
7. Remove from heat and stir in grated Parmesan cheese.
8. Season with salt and pepper to taste.
9. Serve the spinach mushroom risotto as a comforting dish.

Nutritional Information (per serving):
Cal: 420 | Carbs: 74g | Pro: 9g | Fat: 10g | Sugars: 2g | Fiber: 3g | Sodium: 530mg

4. Lemon Herb Couscous

Preparation time: 10 minutes
Preparation time: 10 minutes
Servings: 2

Ingredients:

* 1 cup whole wheat couscous
* 1 1/4 cups low-sodium vegetable broth
* Zest of 1 lemon
* 2 tablespoons chopped fresh parsley
* 1 tablespoon chopped fresh mint

- 2 tablespoons extra virgin olive oil
- Salt and pepper to taste

Instructions:

1. In a pot, bring vegetable broth to a boil.
2. Stir in whole wheat couscous, cover, and remove from heat. Let it sit for about 5 minutes.
3. Fluff the couscous with a fork.
4. Add lemon zest, chopped parsley, chopped mint, extra virgin olive oil, salt, and pepper.
5. Toss the ingredients to combine.
6. Serve the lemon herb couscous as a light and flavorful side.

Nutritional Information (per serving):
Cal: 320 | Carbs: 56g | Pro: 7g | Fat: 8g | Sugars: 1g | Fiber: 8g | Sodium: 320mg

5. Ratatouille with Polenta

Preparation time: 15 minutes
Preparation time: 30 minutes
Servings: 2

Ingredients:

- 1 small eggplant, diced
- 1 small zucchini, diced
- 1 small red bell pepper, diced
- 1 small yellow bell pepper, diced
- 1/2 onion, diced
- 1 can (14 oz) diced tomatoes
- 1/2 teaspoon dried thyme
- 1/2 cup cooked polenta
- Salt and pepper to taste

Instructions:

1. In a skillet, heat a tablespoon of olive oil over medium heat.
2. Add diced eggplant, zucchini, red bell pepper, yellow bell pepper, and onion. Sauté for about 5 minutes, until slightly softened.
3. Stir in diced tomatoes and dried thyme. Simmer for another 15-20 minutes, until the vegetables are tender.
4. Season with salt and pepper to taste.
5. Serve the ratatouille over cooked polenta.

Nutritional Information (per serving):
Cal: 250 | Carbs: 57g | Pro: 5g | Fat: 2g | Sugars: 14g | Fiber: 12g | Sodium: 500mg

6. Zucchini Noodle Stir Fry

Preparation time: 10 minutes
Preparation time: 10 minutes
Servings: 2

Ingredients:

- 2 medium zucchinis, spiralized into noodles
- 1 red bell pepper, thinly sliced
- 1 carrot, julienned
- 2 cloves garlic, minced
- 2 tablespoons low-sodium soy sauce
- 1 tablespoon sesame oil
- 1 tablespoon chopped fresh cilantro
- Salt and pepper to taste

Instructions:

1. In a large skillet, heat sesame oil over medium heat.
2. Add minced garlic and sauté for about 1 minute, until fragrant.
3. Add spiralized zucchini noodles, sliced red bell pepper, and julienned carrot. Stir-fry for about 3-4 minutes, until the vegetables are tender-crisp.
4. Drizzle low-sodium soy sauce over the stir-fry.
5. Season with salt and pepper to taste.
6. Garnish with chopped cilantro before serving.

Nutritional Information (per serving):
Cal: 150 | Carbs: 12g | Pro: 3g | Fat: 10g | Sugars: 6g | Fiber: 3g | Sodium: 420mg

7. Mediterranean Lentil Soup

Preparation time: 10 minutes
Preparation time: 25 minutes
Servings: 2

Ingredients:

- 1 cup brown lentils, rinsed and drained
- 1 carrot, diced
- 1 celery stalk, diced
- 1/2 onion, chopped
- 2 cloves garlic, minced
- 4 cups low-sodium vegetable broth
- 1 teaspoon dried oregano
- Salt and pepper to taste

Instructions:

1. In a pot, heat a tablespoon of olive oil over medium heat.
2. Add chopped onion and minced garlic. Sauté for about 2 minutes, until fragrant.
3. Stir in diced carrot and celery. Sauté for another 3 minutes.
4. Add brown lentils, dried oregano, and low-sodium vegetable broth.
5. Bring the mixture to a boil, then reduce the heat to low, cover, and simmer for about 20-25 minutes, until the lentils are tender.
6. Season with salt and pepper to taste.
7. Serve the Mediterranean lentil soup as a nouri-

-shing dish.

8. Stuffed Eggplant Boats

Preparation time: 15 minutes
Preparation time: 35 minutes
Servings: 2

Ingredients:

- 1 medium eggplant
- 1/2 cup cooked quinoa
- 1/2 cup diced tomatoes
- 1/4 cup crumbled feta cheese
- 2 tablespoons chopped fresh parsley
- 1 tablespoon extra virgin olive oil
- Salt and pepper to taste

Instructions:

1. Preheat the oven to 375°F (190°C).
2. Cut the eggplant in half lengthwise. Scoop out the flesh, leaving about a 1/2-inch shell.
3. Chop the eggplant flesh and sauté in olive oil with diced tomatoes for about 5 minutes.
4. Mix the sautéed mixture with cooked quinoa, crumbled feta cheese, chopped parsley, salt, and pepper.
5. Stuff the eggplant shells with the quinoa mixture.
6. Place the stuffed eggplant boats in a baking dish.
7. Bake in the preheated oven for about 25-30 minutes, until the eggplant is tender.
8. Serve the stuffed eggplant boats as a satisfying dish.

Nutritional Information (per serving):
Cal: 260 | Carbs: 30g | Pro: 8g | Fat: 12g | Sugars: 8g | Fiber: 9g | Sodium: 330mg

9. Farro Vegetable Pilaf

Preparation time: 10 minutes
Preparation time: 25 minutes
Servings: 2

Ingredients:

- 1/2 cup farro
- 1 cup low-sodium vegetable broth
- 1 carrot, diced
- 1/2 zucchini, diced
- 1/4 red onion, finely chopped
- 1 tablespoon chopped fresh parsley
- 2 tablespoons extra virgin olive oil
- Salt and pepper to taste

Instructions:

1. In a pot, bring low-sodium vegetable broth to a boil.
2. Stir in farro, cover, and simmer for about 20-25 minutes, until the farro is tender.
3. In a skillet, heat olive oil over medium heat.
4. Add diced carrot, diced zucchini, and finely chopped red onion. Sauté for about 5 minutes, until the vegetables are softened.
5. Combine the cooked farro with the sautéed vegetables in a bowl.
6. Stir in chopped parsley, salt, and pepper.
7. Serve the farro vegetable pilaf as a nourishing dish.

Nutritional Information (per serving):
Cal: 280 | Carbs: 45g | Pro: 6g | Fat: 10g | Sugars: 4g | Fiber: 7g | Sodium: 300mg

10. Tomato Basil Bulgur

Preparation time: 10 minutes
Preparation time: 15 minutes
Servings: 2

Ingredients:

- 1 cup bulgur
- 2 cups low-sodium vegetable broth
- 1 cup diced tomatoes
- 1/4 cup chopped fresh basil
- 2 tablespoons extra virgin olive oil
- Salt and pepper to taste

Instructions:

1. In a pot, bring low-sodium vegetable broth to a boil.
2. Stir in bulgur, cover, and simmer for about 10-15 minutes, until the bulgur is tender and the liquid is absorbed.
3. Fluff the cooked bulgur with a fork.
4. Stir in diced tomatoes, chopped fresh basil, extra virgin olive oil, salt, and pepper.
5. Toss the ingredients to combine.
6. Serve the tomato basil bulgur as a flavorful side.

Nutritional Information (per serving):
Cal: 280 | Carbs: 45g | Pro: 8g | Fat: 9g | Sugars: 3g | Fiber: 10g | Sodium: 400mg

11. Roasted Vegetable Quinoa

Preparation time: 15 minutes
Preparation time: 25 minutes
Servings: 2

Ingredients:

- 1 cup cooked quinoa
- 1 cup mixed vegetables (bell peppers, zucchini, eggplant), diced
- 2 tablespoons extra virgin olive oil
- 1 teaspoon dried oregano
- Salt and pepper to taste

Instructions:

1. Preheat the oven to 400°F (200°C).
2. Toss mixed vegetables with extra virgin olive oil, dried oregano, salt, and pepper.
3. Spread the vegetables on a baking sheet in a single layer.
4. Roast in the preheated oven for about 20-25 minutes, until the vegetables are tender and slightly caramelized.
5. Mix the roasted vegetables with cooked quinoa.
6. Serve the roasted vegetable quinoa as a hearty dish.

Nutritional Information (per serving):
Cal: 350 | Carbs: 47g | Pro: 7g | Fat: 15g | Sugars: 4g | Fiber: 8g | Sodium: 40mg

12. Greek Style Rice

Preparation time: 10 minutes
Preparation time: 20 minutes
Servings: 2

Ingredients:

- 1 cup long-grain brown rice
- 2 cups low-sodium vegetable broth
- 1/2 cup diced tomatoes
- 1/4 cup chopped Kalamata olives
- 1/4 cup crumbled feta cheese
- 1 tablespoon chopped fresh parsley
- 2 tablespoons extra virgin olive oil
- Salt and pepper to taste

Instructions:

1. In a pot, bring low-sodium vegetable broth to a boil.
2. Stir in brown rice, cover, and simmer for about 15-20 minutes, until the rice is tender and the liquid is absorbed.
3. Fluff the cooked rice with a fork.
4. Stir in diced tomatoes, chopped Kalamata olives, crumbled feta cheese, chopped parsley, extra virgin olive oil, salt, and pepper.
5. Toss the ingredients to combine.
6. Serve the Greek style rice as a flavorful side.

Nutritional Information (per serving):
Cal: 380 | Carbs: 57g | Pro: 8g | Fat: 14g | Sugars: 3g | Fiber: 4g | Sodium: 630mg

13. Caprese Orzo Salad

Preparation time: 10 minutes
Preparation time: 10 minutes
Servings: 2

Ingredients:

- 1 cup whole wheat orzo pasta
- 1 cup cherry tomatoes, halved
- 1/2 cup fresh mozzarella balls, halved
- 1/4 cup chopped fresh basil
- 2 tablespoons extra virgin olive oil
- 1 tablespoon balsamic glaze
- Salt and pepper to taste

Instructions:

1. Cook whole wheat orzo pasta according to package instructions. Drain and let it cool.
2. In a bowl, combine cooked orzo pasta, cherry tomatoes, fresh mozzarella balls, chopped fresh basil, extra virgin olive oil, salt, and pepper.
3. Drizzle balsamic glaze over the salad.
4. Toss the ingredients to combine.
5. Serve the Caprese orzo salad as a delightful side.

Nutritional Information (per serving):
Cal: 320 | Carbs: 40g | Pro: 11g | Fat: 14g | Sugars: 4g | Fiber: 5g | Sodium: 200mg

14. Spaghetti Squash Primavera

Preparation time: 15 minutes
Preparation time: 40 minutes
Servings: 2

Ingredients:

- 1 medium spaghetti squash
- 1/2 cup diced tomatoes
- 1/2 cup diced bell peppers
- 1/2 cup diced zucchini
- 2 cloves garlic, minced
- 2 tablespoons extra virgin olive oil
- 1 tablespoon chopped fresh basil
- Salt and pepper to taste

Instructions:

1. Preheat the oven to 375°F (190°C).
2. Cut the spaghetti squash in half lengthwise and scoop out the seeds.
3. Place the squash halves cut side down on a baking sheet.
4. Bake in the preheated oven for about 30-40 minutes, until the squash strands can be easily separated with a fork.
5. In a skillet, heat extra virgin olive oil over medium heat.

6. Add minced garlic and sauté for about 1 minute, until fragrant.
7. Add diced tomatoes, diced bell peppers, and diced zucchini. Sauté for about 5 minutes, until the vegetables are tender.
8. Use a fork to separate the spaghetti squash strands and add them to the skillet.
9. Toss the squash strands with the sautéed vegetables.
10. Season with chopped fresh basil, salt, and pepper.
11. Serve the spaghetti squash primavera as a light and flavorful dish.

Nutritional Information (per serving):
Cal: 220 | Carbs: 28g | Pro: 4g | Fat: 12g | Sugars: 9g | Fiber: 6g | Sodium: 60mg

15. Mediterranean Barley Bowl

Preparation time: 15 minutes
Preparation time: 40 minutes
Servings: 2

Ingredients:

- 1/2 cup pearl barley
- 1 1/4 cups low-sodium vegetable broth
- 1/2 cup diced cucumbers
- 1/2 cup diced red bell peppers
- 1/4 cup diced red onion
- 1/4 cup chopped fresh parsley
- 2 tablespoons extra virgin olive oil
- 2 tablespoons lemon juice
- Salt and pepper to taste

Instructions:

1. In a pot, bring low-sodium vegetable broth to a boil.
2. Stir in pearl barley, cover, and simmer for about 30-40 minutes, until the barley is tender and the liquid is absorbed.
3. Fluff the cooked barley with a fork.
4. In a bowl, combine cooked barley, diced cucumbers, diced red bell peppers, diced red onion, chopped fresh parsley, extra virgin olive oil, lemon juice, salt, and pepper.
5. Toss the ingredients to combine.
6. Serve the Mediterranean barley bowl as a hearty and satisfying dish.

Nutritional Information (per serving):
Cal: 320 | Carbs: 55g | Pro: 6g | Fat: 9g | Sugars: 4g | Fiber: 10g | Sodium: 340mg

16. Ratatouille Stuffed Bell Peppers

Preparation time: 15 minutes
Preparation time: 35 minutes

Servings: 2

Ingredients:

- 2 large bell peppers, halved and seeds removed
- 1 cup diced eggplant
- 1 cup diced zucchini
- 1/2 cup diced red onion
- 1 cup diced tomatoes
- 1 teaspoon dried thyme
- 2 tablespoons extra virgin olive oil
- Salt and pepper to taste

Instructions:

1. Preheat the oven to 375°F (190°C).
2. In a skillet, heat extra virgin olive oil over medium heat.
3. Add diced eggplant, diced zucchini, diced red onion, and dried thyme. Sauté for about 5 minutes, until slightly softened.
4. Stir in diced tomatoes and sauté for another 2-3 minutes.
5. Stuff the halved bell peppers with the sautéed ratatouille mixture.
6. Place the stuffed bell peppers in a baking dish.
7. Bake in the preheated oven for about 25-30 minutes, until the peppers are tender.
8. Serve the ratatouille stuffed bell peppers as a colorful and flavorful dish.

Nutritional Information (per serving):
Cal: 240 | Carbs: 35g | Pro: 5g | Fat: 11g | Sugars: 14g | Fiber: 9g | Sodium: 180mg

17. Herbed Brown Rice

Preparation time: 10 minutes
Preparation time: 25 minutes
Servings: 2

Ingredients:

- 1 cup long-grain brown rice
- 2 cups low-sodium vegetable broth
- 2 tablespoons chopped fresh herbs (such as parsley, basil, thyme)
- 2 tablespoons extra virgin olive oil
- Salt and pepper to taste

Instructions:

1. In a pot, bring low-sodium vegetable broth to a boil.
2. Stir in brown rice, cover, and simmer for about 20-25 minutes, until the rice is tender and the liquid is absorbed.
3. Fluff the cooked rice with a fork.
4. Stir in chopped fresh herbs and extra virgin olive oil.

5. Season with salt and pepper to taste.
6. Serve the herbed brown rice as a fragrant and flavorful side.

Nutritional Information (per serving):
Cal: 320 | Carbs: 57g | Pro: 6g | Fat: 8g | Sugars: 1g | Fiber: 4g | Sodium: 380mg

18. Eggplant and Farro Casserole

Preparation time: 20 minutes
Preparation time: 45 minutes
Servings: 2

Ingredients:

- 1 cup farro
- 2 cups low-sodium vegetable broth
- 1 medium eggplant, diced
- 1 cup diced tomatoes
- 1/2 cup chopped fresh parsley
- 1/4 cup crumbled feta cheese
- 2 tablespoons extra virgin olive oil
- Salt and pepper to taste

Instructions:

1. In a pot, bring low-sodium vegetable broth to a boil.
2. Stir in farro, cover, and simmer for about 25-30 minutes, until the farro is tender.
3. In a skillet, heat extra virgin olive oil over medium heat.
4. Add diced eggplant and sauté for about 5 minutes, until slightly softened.
5. Stir in diced tomatoes and continue to sauté for another 3-4 minutes.
6. Combine the cooked farro with the sautéed eggplant and tomatoes in a bowl.
7. Stir in chopped fresh parsley, crumbled feta cheese, salt, and pepper.
8. Transfer the mixture to a baking dish and bake in a preheated oven at 375°F (190°C) for about 15-20 minutes, until heated through.
9. Serve the eggplant and farro casserole as a comforting and nutritious dish.

Nutritional Information (per serving):
Cal: 360 | Carbs: 56g | Pro: 11g | Fat: 11g | Sugars: 5g | Fiber: 12g | Sodium: 480mg

19. Cauliflower Fried Rice

Preparation time: 15 minutes
Preparation time: 15 minutes
Servings: 2

Ingredients:

- 2 cups cauliflower florets, riced

- 1/2 cup diced carrots
- 1/2 cup diced bell peppers
- 1/2 cup frozen peas
- 2 cloves garlic, minced
- 2 tablespoons low-sodium soy sauce
- 1 tablespoon sesame oil
- 2 eggs, beaten
- Salt and pepper to taste

Instructions:

1. In a food processor, pulse cauliflower florets until they resemble rice.
2. In a large skillet, heat sesame oil over medium heat.
3. Add minced garlic and sauté for about 1 minute, until fragrant.
4. Add diced carrots and sauté for about 3 minutes, until slightly softened.
5. Push the vegetables to the side of the skillet and pour the beaten eggs into the other side. Scramble the eggs until cooked through.
6. Mix in cauliflower rice, diced bell peppers, and frozen peas.
7. Drizzle low-sodium soy sauce over the cauliflower rice mixture.
8. Stir-fry for about 4-5 minutes, until the vegetables are tender and well combined.
9. Season with salt and pepper to taste.
10. Serve the cauliflower fried rice as a healthier alternative.

Nutritional Information (per serving):
Cal: 220 | Carbs: 23g | Pro: 10g | Fat: 10g | Sugars: 7g | Fiber: 7g | Sodium: 560mg

20. Greek Style Pasta

Preparation time: 10 minutes
Preparation time: 12 minutes
Servings: 2

Ingredients:

- 8 oz whole wheat spaghetti
- 1/2 cup diced tomatoes
- 1/4 cup chopped Kalamata olives
- 1/4 cup crumbled feta cheese
- 2 tablespoons chopped fresh parsley
- 2 tablespoons extra virgin olive oil
- 1 tablespoon lemon juice
- Salt and pepper to taste

Instructions:

1. Cook whole wheat spaghetti according to package instructions. Drain and let it cool.
2. In a bowl, combine cooked spaghetti, diced tomatoes, chopped Kalamata olives, crumbled feta cheese, chopped fresh parsley, extra virgin olive oil, lemon juice, salt, and pepper.

3. Toss the ingredients to combine.
4. Serve the Greek style pasta as a flavorful and satisfying dish.

Nutritional Information (per serving):
Cal: 380 | Carbs: 58g | Pro: 14g | Fat: 11g | Sugars: 3g | Fiber: 10g | Sodium: 420mg

Salads

1. Greek Quinoa Salad

Preparation time: 15 minutes
Servings: 2

Ingredients:

- 1 cup cooked quinoa, cooled
- 1 cup diced cucumber
- 1/2 cup diced red bell pepper
- 1/4 cup chopped red onion
- 1/4 cup crumbled feta cheese
- 2 tablespoons chopped fresh parsley
- 2 tablespoons extra virgin olive oil
- Juice of 1 lemon
- Salt and pepper to taste

Instructions:

1. In a large bowl, combine cooked quinoa, diced cucumber, diced red bell pepper, chopped red onion, crumbled feta cheese, and chopped parsley.
2. In a small bowl, whisk together extra virgin olive oil, lemon juice, salt, and pepper.
3. Drizzle the dressing over the quinoa mixture and toss to combine.
4. Serve the Greek quinoa salad as a refreshing and nutritious dish.

Nutritional Information (per serving):
Cal: 330 | Carbs: 31g | Pro: 10g | Fat: 20g | Sugars: 5g | Fiber: 4g | Sodium: 320mg

2. Mediterranean Chickpea Salad

Preparation time: 10 minutes
Servings: 2

Ingredients:

- 1 can (15 oz) chickpeas, drained and rinsed
- 1 cup diced cucumber
- 1 cup diced tomatoes
- 1/4 cup diced red onion
- 2 tablespoons chopped fresh parsley
- 2 tablespoons extra virgin olive oil
- Juice of 1 lemon
- Salt and pepper to taste

Instructions:

1. In a bowl, combine chickpeas, diced cucumber, diced tomatoes, diced red onion, and chopped parsley.
2. In a small bowl, whisk together extra virgin olive oil, lemon juice, salt, and pepper.
3. Drizzle the dressing over the chickpea mixture and toss to combine.
4. Serve the Mediterranean chickpea salad for a

satisfying and protein-rich meal.

Nutritional Information (per serving):
Cal: 300 | Carbs: 38g | Pro: 10g | Fat: 13g | Sugars: 6g | Fiber: 10g | Sodium: 320mg

3. Tomato Basil Salad

Preparation time: 10 minutes
Servings: 2

Ingredients:

- 2 cups diced tomatoes
- 1/4 cup chopped fresh basil
- 2 tablespoons extra virgin olive oil
- 2 tablespoons balsamic vinegar
- 1/4 cup crumbled feta cheese
- Salt and pepper to taste

Instructions:

1. In a bowl, combine diced tomatoes, chopped basil, extra virgin olive oil, and balsamic vinegar.
2. Gently mix in crumbled feta cheese.
3. Season with salt and pepper to taste.
4. Serve the tomato basil salad as a simple and flavorful side dish.

Nutritional Information (per serving):
Cal: 170 | Carbs: 10g | Pro: 4g | Fat: 14g | Sugars: 6g | Fiber: 2g | Sodium: 220mg

4. Cucumber Feta Salad

Preparation time: 10 minutes
Servings: 2

Ingredients:

- 2 cups diced cucumber
- 1/4 cup diced red onion
- 1/4 cup crumbled feta cheese
- 2 tablespoons chopped fresh dill
- 2 tablespoons extra virgin olive oil
- Juice of 1 lemon
- Salt and pepper to taste

Instructions:

1. In a bowl, combine diced cucumber, diced red onion, crumbled feta cheese, and chopped dill.
2. In a small bowl, whisk together extra virgin olive oil, lemon juice, salt, and pepper.
3. Drizzle the dressing over the cucumber mixture and toss to combine.
4. Serve the cucumber feta salad for a light and refreshing dish.

Nutritional Information (per serving):
Cal: 180 | Carbs: 10g | Pro: 4g | Fat: 15g | Sugars: 4g | Fiber: 2g | Sodium: 250mg

5. Tuna White Bean Salad

Preparation time: 10 minutes
Servings: 2

Ingredients:

- 1 can (5 oz) tuna in water, drained
- 1 can (15 oz) white beans, drained and rinsed
- 1/4 cup chopped red onion
- 2 tablespoons chopped fresh parsley
- 2 tablespoons extra virgin olive oil
- Juice of 1 lemon
- Salt and pepper to taste

Instructions:

1. In a bowl, flake the drained tuna and combine it with white beans, chopped red onion, and chopped parsley.
2. In a small bowl, whisk together extra virgin olive oil, lemon juice, salt, and pepper.
3. Drizzle the dressing over the tuna and white bean mixture and toss to combine.
4. Serve the tuna white bean salad for a protein-packed and satisfying meal.

Nutritional Information (per serving):
Cal: 280 | Carbs: 30g | Pro: 20g | Fat: 10g | Sugars: 1g | Fiber: 10g | Sodium: 520mg

6. Greek Salad Wraps

Preparation time: 15 minutes
Servings: 2

Ingredients:

- 4 large lettuce leaves
- 1 cup diced cucumber
- 1/2 cup diced tomatoes
- 1/4 cup diced red onion
- 1/4 cup crumbled feta cheese
- 2 tablespoons chopped fresh parsley
- 2 tablespoons extra virgin olive oil
- Juice of 1 lemon
- Salt and pepper to taste

Instructions:

1. Lay out lettuce leaves and divide diced cucumber, diced tomatoes, diced red onion, crumbled feta cheese, and chopped parsley between them.
2. In a small bowl, whisk together extra virgin olive

oil, lemon juice, salt, and pepper.
3. Drizzle the dressing over the fillings in each lettuce leaf.
4. Roll up the lettuce leaves to create Greek salad wraps.
5. Serve the wraps as a convenient and low-carb lunch option.

Nutritional Information (per serving):
Cal: 190 | Carbs: 9g | Pro: 5g | Fat: 15g | Sugars: 4g | Fiber: 3g | Sodium: 300mg

7. Minty Watermelon Salad

Preparation time: 10 minutes
Servings: 2

Ingredients:

- 2 cups diced watermelon
- 1/4 cup crumbled feta cheese
- 2 tablespoons chopped fresh mint
- 2 tablespoons extra virgin olive oil
- Juice of 1 lime
- Salt and pepper to taste

Instructions:

1. In a bowl, combine diced watermelon, crumbled feta cheese, and chopped mint.
2. In a small bowl, whisk together extra virgin olive oil, lime juice, salt, and pepper.
3. Drizzle the dressing over the watermelon mixture and toss to combine.
4. Serve the minty watermelon salad for a refreshing and hydrating dish.

Nutritional Information (per serving):
Cal: 180 | Carbs: 14g | Pro: 4g | Fat: 13g | Sugars: 10g | Fiber: 1g | Sodium: 200mg

8. Orzo Spinach Salad

Preparation time: 15 minutes
Servings: 2

Ingredients:

- 1 cup cooked orzo pasta, cooled
- 2 cups baby spinach
- 1/4 cup crumbled feta cheese
- 2 tablespoons chopped fresh dill
- 2 tablespoons extra virgin olive oil
- Juice of 1 lemon
- Salt and pepper to taste

Instructions:

1. In a large bowl, combine cooked orzo pasta,

baby spinach, crumbled feta cheese, and chopped dill.
2. In a small bowl, whisk together extra virgin olive oil, lemon juice, salt, and pepper.
3. Drizzle the dressing over the orzo mixture and toss to combine.
4. Serve the orzo spinach salad as a satisfying and balanced meal.

Nutritional Information (per serving):
Cal: 300 | Carbs: 30g | Pro: 7g | Fat: 18g | Sugars: 2g | Fiber: 3g | Sodium: 330mg

9. Roasted Beet Salad

Preparation time: 10 minutes
Cook time: 45 minutes
Servings: 2

Ingredients:

- 2 medium beets, roasted and diced
- 2 cups arugula
- 1/4 cup crumbled goat cheese
- 2 tablespoons chopped walnuts
- 2 tablespoons balsamic vinegar
- 2 tablespoons extra virgin olive oil
- Salt and pepper to taste

Instructions:

1. Preheat the oven to 400°F (200°C).
2. Wrap the beets in foil and roast for about 40-45 minutes, until tender.
3. Let the beets cool, then peel and dice them.
4. In a bowl, combine diced roasted beets, arugula, crumbled goat cheese, and chopped walnuts.
5. In a small bowl, whisk together balsamic vinegar, extra virgin olive oil, salt, and pepper.
6. Drizzle the dressing over the salad and toss to combine.
7. Serve the roasted beet salad as a nutrient-rich and flavorful dish.

Nutritional Information (per serving):
Cal: 270 | Carbs: 18g | Pro: 6g | Fat: 20g | Sugars: 10g | Fiber: 4g | Sodium: 220mg

10. Caprese Salad Skewers

Preparation time: 15 minutes
Servings: 2

Ingredients:

- 12 cherry tomatoes
- 12 fresh mozzarella balls
- 12 fresh basil leaves
- 2 tablespoons balsamic glaze
- 2 tablespoons extra virgin olive oil

- Salt and pepper to taste

Instructions:

1. Thread cherry tomatoes, fresh mozzarella balls, and fresh basil leaves onto skewers.
2. Arrange the skewers on a serving plate.
3. Drizzle balsamic glaze and extra virgin olive oil over the skewers.
4. Season with salt and pepper to taste.
5. Serve the Caprese salad skewers as a delightful and elegant appetizer.

Nutritional Information (per serving):
Cal: 190 | Carbs: 6g | Pro: 10g | Fat: 14g | Sugars: 4g | Fiber: 1g | Sodium: 220mg

11. Lemon Herb Couscous Salad

Preparation time: 15 minutes
Cook time: 10 minutes
Servings: 2

Ingredients:

- 1 cup cooked whole wheat couscous, cooled
- 1 cup diced cucumbers
- 1 cup diced bell peppers
- 2 tablespoons chopped fresh mint
- 2 tablespoons chopped fresh parsley
- 2 tablespoons extra virgin olive oil
- Juice of 1 lemon
- Salt and pepper to taste

Instructions:

1. In a bowl, combine cooked couscous, diced cucumbers, diced bell peppers, chopped mint, and chopped parsley.
2. In a small bowl, whisk together extra virgin olive oil, lemon juice, salt, and pepper.
3. Drizzle the dressing over the couscous mixture and toss to combine.
4. Serve the lemon herb couscous salad as a light and flavorful dish.

Nutritional Information (per serving):
Cal: 260 | Carbs: 38g | Pro: 5g | Fat: 11g | Sugars: 4g | Fiber: 6g | Sodium: 200mg

12. Arugula Pomegranate Salad

Preparation time: 10 minutes
Servings: 2

Ingredients:

- 4 cups baby arugula
- 1/2 cup pomegranate seeds
- 1/4 cup crumbled goat cheese

- 2 tablespoons chopped toasted walnuts
- 2 tablespoons balsamic vinegar
- 2 tablespoons extra virgin olive oil
- Salt and pepper to taste

Instructions:

1. In a large bowl, combine baby arugula, pomegranate seeds, crumbled goat cheese, and chopped toasted walnuts.
2. In a small bowl, whisk together balsamic vinegar, extra virgin olive oil, salt, and pepper.
3. Drizzle the dressing over the salad and toss to combine.
4. Serve the arugula pomegranate salad for a vibrant and antioxidant-rich meal.

Nutritional Information (per serving):
Cal: 230 | Carbs: 14g | Pro: 6g | Fat: 18g | Sugars: 7g | Fiber: 3g | Sodium: 220mg

13. Zesty Shrimp Salad

Preparation time: 10 minutes
Cook time: 5 minutes
Servings: 2

Ingredients:

- 8 oz shrimp, peeled and deveined
- 4 cups mixed salad greens
- 1/4 cup diced red onion
- 2 tablespoons chopped fresh cilantro
- 2 tablespoons extra virgin olive oil
- Juice of 1 lime
- 1 teaspoon chili powder
- Salt and pepper to taste

Instructions:

1. Preheat a skillet over medium-high heat.
2. Season shrimp with chili powder, salt, and pepper.
3. Cook shrimp for about 2-3 minutes on each side, until pink and opaque.
4. In a large bowl, combine mixed salad greens, diced red onion, and chopped cilantro.
5. In a small bowl, whisk together extra virgin olive oil and lime juice.
6. Drizzle the dressing over the salad greens and toss to combine.
7. Arrange cooked shrimp over the salad.
8. Serve the zesty shrimp salad for a protein-packed and zingy meal.

Nutritional Information (per serving):
Cal: 280 | Carbs: 6g | Pro: 22g | Fat: 18g | Sugars: 2g | Fiber: 2g | Sodium: 350mg

14. Avocado Tomato Salad

Preparation time: 10 minutes
Servings: 2

Ingredients:

- 1 large avocado, diced
- 1 cup diced tomatoes
- 1/4 cup diced red onion
- 2 tablespoons chopped fresh cilantro
- 2 tablespoons extra virgin olive oil
- Juice of 1 lime
- Salt and pepper to taste

Instructions:

1. In a bowl, combine diced avocado, diced tomatoes, diced red onion, and chopped cilantro.
2. In a small bowl, whisk together extra virgin olive oil and lime juice.
3. Drizzle the dressing over the avocado mixture and toss to combine.
4. Serve the avocado tomato salad for a creamy and refreshing dish.

Nutritional Information (per serving):
Cal: 240 | Carbs: 12g | Pro: 2g | Fat: 22g | Sugars: 3g | Fiber: 7g | Sodium: 15mg

15. Spinach Berry Salad

Preparation time: 10 minutes
Servings: 2

Ingredients:

- 4 cups baby spinach
- 1 cup mixed berries (strawberries, blueberries, raspberries)
- 1/4 cup crumbled goat cheese
- 2 tablespoons chopped toasted almonds
- 2 tablespoons balsamic vinegar
- 2 tablespoons extra virgin olive oil
- Salt and pepper to taste

Instructions:

1. In a large bowl, combine baby spinach, mixed berries, crumbled goat cheese, and chopped toasted almonds.
2. In a small bowl, whisk together balsamic vinegar, extra virgin olive oil, salt, and pepper.
3. Drizzle the dressing over the salad and toss to combine.
4. Serve the spinach berry salad for a nutrient-packed and colorful meal.

Nutritional Information (per serving):
Cal: 220 | Carbs: 14g | Pro: 6g | Fat: 16g | Sugars:

7g | Fiber: 5g | Sodium: 150mg

16. Grilled Eggplant Salad

Preparation time: 15 minutes
Preparation time: 10 minutes
Servings: 2

Ingredients:

- 1 medium eggplant, sliced
- 2 cups mixed salad greens
- 1/4 cup crumbled feta cheese
- 2 tablespoons chopped fresh basil
- 2 tablespoons extra virgin olive oil
- Juice of 1 lemon
- Salt and pepper to taste

Instructions:

1. Preheat a grill or grill pan over medium heat.
2. Brush eggplant slices with olive oil and grill for about 3-4 minutes on each side, until tender and grill marks appear.
3. In a large bowl, combine mixed salad greens, crumbled feta cheese, and chopped basil.
4. In a small bowl, whisk together extra virgin olive oil and lemon juice.
5. Drizzle the dressing over the salad greens and toss to combine.
6. Arrange grilled eggplant slices over the salad.
7. Serve the grilled eggplant salad for a smoky and satisfying dish.

Nutritional Information (per serving):
Cal: 240 | Carbs: 20g | Pro: 6g | Fat: 18g | Sugars: 10g | Fiber: 8g | Sodium: 260mg

17. Kale Quinoa Salad

Preparation time: 15 minutes
Preparation time: 15 minutes
Servings: 2

Ingredients:

- 4 cups chopped kale leaves
- 1 cup cooked quinoa, cooled
- 1/4 cup dried cranberries
- 2 tablespoons chopped toasted pecans
- 2 tablespoons balsamic vinegar
- 2 tablespoons extra virgin olive oil
- Salt and pepper to taste

Instructions:

1. In a large bowl, massage chopped kale leaves with a small amount of olive oil until slightly softened.
2. Add cooked quinoa, dried cranberries, and

chopped toasted pecans to the bowl.
3. In a small bowl, whisk together balsamic vinegar, extra virgin olive oil, salt, and pepper.
4. Drizzle the dressing over the salad and toss to combine.
5. Serve the kale quinoa salad as a hearty and nutritious meal.

Nutritional Information (per serving):
Cal: 300 | Carbs: 34g | Pro: 6g | Fat: 16g | Sugars: 9g | Fiber: 5g | Sodium: 180mg

18. Roasted Red Pepper Salad

Preparation time: 10 minutes
Preparation time: 15 minutes
Servings: 2

Ingredients:

- 2 large red bell peppers
- 2 cups mixed salad greens
- 1/4 cup crumbled goat cheese
- 2 tablespoons chopped fresh parsley
- 2 tablespoons extra virgin olive oil
- Juice of 1 lemon
- Salt and pepper to taste

Instructions:

1. Preheat the oven to 400°F (200°C).
2. Place whole red bell peppers on a baking sheet and roast for about 15-20 minutes, until charred and tender.
3. Remove peppers from the oven, let them cool slightly, then peel, seed, and slice them.
4. In a large bowl, combine mixed salad greens, crumbled goat cheese, and chopped parsley.
5. In a small bowl, whisk together extra virgin olive oil, lemon juice, salt, and pepper.
6. Drizzle the dressing over the salad greens and toss to combine.
7. Arrange roasted red pepper slices over the salad.
8. Serve the roasted red pepper salad for a flavorful and colorful dish.

Nutritional Information (per serving):
Cal: 210 | Carbs: 9g | Pro: 5g | Fat: 18g | Sugars: 6g | Fiber: 3g | Sodium: 230mg

19. Artichoke Heart Salad

Preparation time: 10 minutes
Servings: 2

Ingredients:

- 2 cups baby spinach
- 1 cup canned artichoke hearts, drained and quartered

- 1/4 cup chopped sun-dried tomatoes
- 2 tablespoons chopped fresh basil
- 2 tablespoons extra virgin olive oil
- Juice of 1 lemon
- Salt and pepper to taste

Instructions:

1. In a large bowl, combine baby spinach, artichoke hearts, chopped sun-dried tomatoes, and chopped basil.
2. In a small bowl, whisk together extra virgin olive oil, lemon juice, salt, and pepper.
3. Drizzle the dressing over the salad and toss to combine.
4. Serve the artichoke heart salad for a tangy and savory meal.

Nutritional Information (per serving):
Cal: 200 | Carbs: 12g | Pro: 5g | Fat: 15g | Sugars: 3g | Fiber: 5g | Sodium: 280mg

20. Mango Avocado Salad

Preparation time: 10 minutes
Servings: 2

Ingredients:

- 1 large mango, peeled and diced
- 1 large avocado, diced
- 1/4 cup diced red onion
- 2 tablespoons chopped fresh cilantro
- 2 tablespoons extra virgin olive oil
- Juice of 1 lime
- Salt and pepper to taste

Instructions:

1. In a bowl, combine diced mango, diced avocado, diced red onion, and chopped cilantro.
2. In a small bowl, whisk together extra virgin olive oil and lime juice.
3. Drizzle the dressing over the mango and avocado mixture and toss to combine.
4. Serve the mango avocado salad for a tropical and satisfying dish.

Nutritional Information (per serving):
Cal: 270 | Carbs: 22g | Pro: 2g | Fat: 21g | Sugars: 14g | Fiber: 7g | Sodium: 15mg

Snacks and Appetizers

1. Olive Tapenade Crostini

Preparation time: 10 minutes
Servings: 2

Ingredients:

- 1 cup pitted Kalamata olives
- 2 cloves garlic, minced
- 2 tablespoons extra virgin olive oil
- 1 teaspoon lemon juice
- 1 teaspoon capers
- 1 tablespoon chopped fresh parsley
- Slices of whole grain baguette

Instructions:

1. In a food processor, combine olives, garlic, olive oil, lemon juice, and capers. Pulse until a coarse paste forms.
2. Stir in chopped parsley.
3. Toast the slices of whole grain baguette until golden and crispy.
4. Spread olive tapenade over each slice of toasted baguette.
5. Serve as an appetizer or snack.

Nutritional Information (per serving):
Cal: 150 | Carbs: 15g | Pro: 2g | Fat: 10g | Sugars: 1g | Fiber: 3g | Sodium: 480mg

2. Greek Yogurt Dip

Preparation time: 5 minutes
Servings: 2

Ingredients:

- 1 cup Greek yogurt
- 1 tablespoon extra virgin olive oil
- 1 teaspoon dried dill
- 1 teaspoon lemon juice
- 1 clove garlic, minced
- Salt and pepper to taste
- Fresh vegetables for dipping (carrots, cucumber, bell peppers)

Instructions:

1. In a bowl, combine Greek yogurt, olive oil, dried dill, lemon juice, and minced garlic.
2. Mix well and season with salt and pepper to taste.
3. Serve the yogurt dip with fresh vegetable sticks for dipping.

Nutritional Information (per serving):
Cal: 120 | Carbs: 8g | Pro: 10g | Fat: 6g | Sugars: 6g | Fiber: 1g | Sodium: 80mg

3. Hummus Stuffed Peppers

Preparation time: 15 minutes
Servings: 2

Ingredients:

- 2 large bell peppers (red, yellow, or orange)
- 1/2 cup prepared hummus
- 1/4 cup diced cucumbers
- 1/4 cup diced tomatoes
- 2 tablespoons chopped Kalamata olives
- Fresh parsley leaves for garnish
- Olive oil for drizzling

Instructions:

1. Cut the tops off the bell peppers and remove the seeds and membranes.
2. In a bowl, mix hummus, diced cucumbers, diced tomatoes, and chopped Kalamata olives.
3. Stuff the bell peppers with the hummus mixture.
4. Drizzle with olive oil and garnish with fresh parsley leaves.
5. Serve as a colorful and flavorful appetizer.

Nutritional Information (per serving):
Cal: 150 | Carbs: 15g | Pro: 5g | Fat: 8g | Sugars: 4g | Fiber: 4g | Sodium: 260mg

4. Cucumber Feta Bites

Preparation time: 10 minutes
Servings: 2

Ingredients:

- 1 cucumber
- 1/4 cup crumbled feta cheese
- 2 tablespoons chopped fresh mint
- 1 tablespoon extra virgin olive oil
- 1 teaspoon lemon juice
- Black pepper to taste

Instructions:

1. Slice the cucumber into rounds.
2. In a bowl, combine crumbled feta cheese, chopped fresh mint, olive oil, and lemon juice. Mix well.
3. Place a teaspoon of the feta mixture on top of each cucumber slice.
4. Sprinkle with black pepper.
5. Serve the cucumber feta bites as a light and refreshing appetizer.

Nutritional Information (per serving):
Cal: 90 | Carbs: 4g | Pro: 3g | Fat: 7g | Sugars: 2g | Fiber: 1g | Sodium: 180mg

5. Spinach Artichoke Dip

Preparation time: 20 minutes
Servings: 2

Ingredients:

* 1 cup chopped spinach (fresh or frozen, thawed and drained)
* 1/2 cup chopped artichoke hearts (canned or frozen, thawed)
* 1/4 cup Greek yogurt
* 1/4 cup grated Parmesan cheese
* 1/4 cup shredded mozzarella cheese
* 1 clove garlic, minced
* Salt and pepper to taste

Instructions:

1. Preheat the oven to 375°F (190°C).
2. In a bowl, combine chopped spinach, chopped artichoke hearts, Greek yogurt, grated Parmesan cheese, shredded mozzarella cheese, and minced garlic.
3. Season with salt and pepper to taste.
4. Transfer the mixture to a baking dish and bake for about 15 minutes, until bubbly and golden on top.
5. Serve the spinach artichoke dip with whole grain pita chips or vegetable sticks.

Nutritional Information (per serving):
Cal: 150 | Carbs: 7g | Pro: 10g | Fat: 9g | Sugars: 2g | Fiber: 2g | Sodium: 450mg

6. Tomato Basil Bruschetta

Preparation time: 15 minutes
Servings: 2

Ingredients:

* 4 slices whole grain baguette
* 2 medium tomatoes, diced
* 1/4 cup fresh basil, chopped
* 1 clove garlic, minced
* 1 tablespoon extra virgin olive oil
* Salt and pepper to taste

Instructions:

1. Preheat the oven to 375°F (190°C).
2. Place the baguette slices on a baking sheet and toast them in the oven until lightly crispy.
3. In a bowl, combine diced tomatoes, chopped fresh basil, minced garlic, and extra virgin olive oil.
4. Season with salt and pepper to taste.
5. Spoon the tomato basil mixture onto the toasted baguette slices.
6. Serve as an appetizer or snack.

Nutritional Information (per serving):
Cal: 120 | Carbs: 15g | Pro: 3g | Fat: 5g | Sugars: 2g | Fiber: 2g | Sodium: 150mg

7. Mediterranean Tuna Salad

Preparation time: 10 minutes
Servings: 2

Ingredients:

* 1 can (5 oz) tuna, drained
* 1/4 cup chopped cucumber
* 1/4 cup chopped tomatoes
* 2 tablespoons chopped Kalamata olives
* 2 tablespoons crumbled feta cheese
* 1 tablespoon extra virgin olive oil
* Lemon juice, to taste

Instructions:

1. In a bowl, combine drained tuna, chopped cucumber, chopped tomatoes, chopped Kalamata olives, and crumbled feta cheese.
2. Drizzle with extra virgin olive oil and a squeeze of lemon juice.
3. Toss gently to combine.
4. Serve the Mediterranean tuna salad on whole grain crackers or lettuce leaves.

Nutritional Information (per serving):
Cal: 170 | Carbs: 6g | Pro: 15g | Fat: 10g | Sugars: 2g | Fiber: 1g | Sodium: 350mg

8. Roasted Red Pepper Hummus

Preparation time: 10 minutes
Servings: 2

Ingredients:

* 1 can (15 oz) chickpeas, drained and rinsed
* 1/4 cup roasted red peppers (from a jar), drained
* 2 tablespoons tahini
* 2 tablespoons lemon juice
* 1 clove garlic, minced
* 1/2 teaspoon ground cumin
* Salt and pepper to taste

Instructions:

1. In a food processor, combine chickpeas, roasted red peppers, tahini, lemon juice, minced garlic, and ground cumin.
2. Blend until smooth, adding a splash of water if needed to achieve desired consistency.
3. Season with salt and pepper to taste.
4. Serve the roasted red pepper hummus with whole grain pita wedges or vegetable sticks.

Nutritional Information (per serving):
Cal: 160 | Carbs: 20g | Pro: 7g | Fat: 7g | Sugars: 3g | Fiber: 6g | Sodium: 300mg

9. Stuffed Grape Leaves

Preparation time: 20 minutes
Servings: 2

Ingredients:

- 10 canned grape leaves, drained
- 1/2 cup cooked quinoa
- 1/4 cup crumbled feta cheese
- 2 tablespoons chopped fresh dill
- 2 tablespoons chopped Kalamata olives
- 1 tablespoon extra virgin olive oil
- Lemon wedges for serving

Instructions:

1. Gently rinse the canned grape leaves and pat them dry.
2. In a bowl, mix cooked quinoa, crumbled feta cheese, chopped fresh dill, and chopped Kalamata olives.
3. Place a spoonful of the quinoa mixture in the center of each grape leaf and fold the sides in, then roll it up.
4. Arrange the stuffed grape leaves on a serving plate.
5. Drizzle with extra virgin olive oil and serve with lemon wedges.

Nutritional Information (per serving):
Cal: 150 | Carbs: 17g | Pro: 5g | Fat: 7g | Sugars: 2g | Fiber: 3g | Sodium: 500mg

10. Feta Cucumber Boats

Preparation time: 10 minutes
Servings: 2

Ingredients:

- 1 cucumber
- 1/4 cup crumbled feta cheese
- 2 tablespoons chopped Kalamata olives
- 2 tablespoons chopped fresh parsley
- 1 tablespoon extra virgin olive oil
- Lemon juice, to taste

Instructions:

1. Cut the cucumber in half lengthwise and scoop out the seeds to create a hollow "boat."
2. In a bowl, combine crumbled feta cheese, chopped Kalamata olives, chopped fresh parsley, extra virgin olive oil, and a squeeze of lemon juice.
3. Fill each cucumber boat with the feta mixture.

4. Serve the feta cucumber boats as a refreshing appetizer.

Nutritional Information (per serving):
Cal: 130 | Carbs: 6g | Pro: 4g | Fat: 10g | Sugars: 3g | Fiber: 2g | Sodium: 300mg

11. Smoked Salmon Rolls

Preparation time: 10 minutes
Servings: 2

Ingredients:

- 4 slices smoked salmon
- 1/4 cup whipped cream cheese
- 2 tablespoons chopped fresh dill
- 2 tablespoons chopped red onion
- Fresh lemon zest, for garnish

Instructions:

1. Lay out the smoked salmon slices on a clean surface.
2. Spread a thin layer of whipped cream cheese on each slice.
3. Sprinkle chopped fresh dill and chopped red onion over the cream cheese.
4. Gently roll up the smoked salmon slices.
5. Arrange the smoked salmon rolls on a serving plate.
6. Garnish with fresh lemon zest.
7. Serve as an elegant and flavorful appetizer.

Nutritional Information (per serving):
Cal: 120 | Carbs: 2g | Pro: 10g | Fat: 8g | Sugars: 1g | Fiber: 0g | Sodium: 400mg

12. Greek Stuffed Mushrooms

Preparation time: 20 minutes
Servings: 2

Ingredients:

- 8 large button mushrooms
- 1/4 cup cooked quinoa
- 1/4 cup crumbled feta cheese
- 2 tablespoons chopped Kalamata olives
- 2 tablespoons chopped fresh parsley
- 1 tablespoon extra virgin olive oil
- Lemon juice, to taste

Instructions:

1. Remove the stems from the mushrooms and gently scoop out some of the centers to create space for the stuffing.
2. In a bowl, mix cooked quinoa, crumbled feta cheese, chopped Kalamata olives, chopped

fresh parsley, extra virgin olive oil, and a squeeze of lemon juice.
3. Spoon the quinoa mixture into the mushroom caps.
4. Place the stuffed mushrooms on a baking sheet.
5. Bake in a preheated oven at 375°F (190°C) for about 15 minutes, or until the mushrooms are tender.
6. Serve the Greek stuffed mushrooms as an appetizer or side dish.

Nutritional Information (per serving):
Cal: 140 | Carbs: 10g | Pro: 6g | Fat: 9g | Sugars: 2g | Fiber: 2g | Sodium: 250mg

13. Spiced Almonds Mix

Preparation time: 5 minutes
Servings: 2

Ingredients:

- 1/2 cup raw almonds
- 1/2 teaspoon ground cumin
- 1/2 teaspoon smoked paprika
- 1/4 teaspoon ground cinnamon
- 1/4 teaspoon ground turmeric
- 1/4 teaspoon salt

Instructions:

1. In a dry skillet over medium heat, toast the raw almonds for a few minutes until fragrant. Let them cool.
2. In a bowl, combine ground cumin, smoked paprika, ground cinnamon, ground turmeric, and salt.
3. Toss the toasted almonds in the spice mixture until coated.
4. Serve the spiced almonds mix as a flavorful and satisfying snack.

Nutritional Information (per serving):
Cal: 160 | Carbs: 6g | Pro: 6g | Fat: 14g | Sugars: 1g | Fiber: 3g | Sodium: 150mg

14. Zucchini Fritters

Preparation time: 20 minutes
Servings: 2

Ingredients:

- 1 medium zucchini, grated
- 1/4 cup crumbled feta cheese
- 1/4 cup whole wheat flour
- 1 egg
- 2 tablespoons chopped fresh dill
- 1 clove garlic, minced

- Salt and pepper to taste

Instructions:

1. Place the grated zucchini in a clean kitchen towel and squeeze out excess moisture.
2. In a bowl, combine grated zucchini, crumbled feta cheese, whole wheat flour, egg, chopped fresh dill, minced garlic, salt, and pepper.
3. Mix until well combined.
4. Heat a non-stick skillet over medium heat and lightly coat with olive oil.
5. Spoon the zucchini mixture onto the skillet to form fritters. Flatten with a spatula.
6. Cook for about 3-4 minutes on each side, or until golden brown.
7. Serve the zucchini fritters with a dollop of Greek yogurt.

Nutritional Information (per serving):
Cal: 150 | Carbs: 13g | Pro: 9g | Fat: 7g | Sugars: 2g | Fiber: 2g | Sodium: 300mg

15. Eggplant Caponata

Preparation time: 15 minutes
Servings: 2

Ingredients:

- 1 small eggplant, diced
- 1/4 cup chopped tomatoes
- 1/4 cup chopped red bell pepper
- 2 tablespoons chopped Kalamata olives
- 1 tablespoon capers
- 1 tablespoon extra virgin olive oil
- 1 tablespoon red wine vinegar
- Fresh basil leaves for garnish

Instructions:

1. In a skillet, heat extra virgin olive oil over medium heat.
2. Add diced eggplant and sauté until softened and lightly browned.
3. Stir in chopped tomatoes, chopped red bell pepper, chopped Kalamata olives, and capers.
4. Cook for a few more minutes until the vegetables are tender.
5. Remove from heat and drizzle with red wine vinegar.
6. Allow the eggplant caponata to cool slightly.
7. Garnish with fresh basil leaves before serving.

Nutritional Information (per serving):
Cal: 120 | Carbs: 12g | Pro: 2g | Fat: 8g | Sugars: 6g | Fiber: 5g | Sodium: 300mg

16. Herbed Quinoa Bites

Preparation time: 15 minutes
Servings: 2

Ingredients:

- 1/2 cup cooked quinoa
- 1/4 cup grated Parmesan cheese
- 2 tablespoons chopped fresh parsley
- 1 green onion, finely chopped
- 1 egg
- Salt and pepper to taste

Instructions:

1. In a bowl, combine cooked quinoa, grated Parmesan cheese, chopped fresh parsley, finely chopped green onion, egg, salt, and pepper.
2. Mix until the ingredients are well combined.
3. Preheat the oven to 375°F (190°C) and line a baking sheet with parchment paper.
4. Using your hands, shape the quinoa mixture into small bite-sized balls.
5. Place the quinoa bites on the prepared baking sheet.
6. Bake for about 15-20 minutes, or until the bites are golden and firm.
7. Serve the herbed quinoa bites with a yogurt-based dipping sauce.

Nutritional Information (per serving):
Cal: 140 | Carbs: 15g | Pro: 9g | Fat: 5g | Sugars: 1g | Fiber: 2g | Sodium: 220mg

17. Lemon Garlic Shrimp Skewers

Preparation time: 15 minutes
Servings: 2

Ingredients:

- 8 large shrimp, peeled and deveined
- 2 tablespoons fresh lemon juice
- 2 cloves garlic, minced
- 1 tablespoon extra virgin olive oil
- 1/2 teaspoon dried oregano
- Salt and pepper to taste
- Wooden skewers, soaked in water

Instructions:

1. In a bowl, mix fresh lemon juice, minced garlic, extra virgin olive oil, dried oregano, salt, and pepper.
2. Add the peeled and deveined shrimp to the marinade and toss to coat.
3. Cover and refrigerate for about 10-15 minutes.
4. Thread the marinated shrimp onto the soaked wooden skewers.

5. Preheat a grill or grill pan over medium-high heat.
6. Grill the shrimp skewers for 2-3 minutes on each side, or until opaque and cooked through.
7. Serve the lemon garlic shrimp skewers with a side of Greek yogurt sauce.

Nutritional Information (per serving):
Cal: 120 | Carbs: 2g | Pro: 16g | Fat: 5g | Sugars: 0g | Fiber: 0g | Sodium: 220mg

18. Yogurt Cucumber Cups

Preparation time: 10 minutes
Servings: 2

Ingredients:

- 1 large cucumber
- 1/2 cup Greek yogurt
- 2 tablespoons chopped fresh dill
- 1 tablespoon chopped red onion
- 1/2 teaspoon lemon zest
- Salt and pepper to taste

Instructions:

1. Cut the cucumber into thick slices, about 1 inch each.
2. Use a spoon to scoop out the center of each cucumber slice, creating a cup-like shape.
3. In a bowl, mix Greek yogurt, chopped fresh dill, chopped red onion, lemon zest, salt, and pepper.
4. Spoon the yogurt mixture into the cucumber cups.
5. Serve the yogurt cucumber cups as a refreshing and light snack.

Nutritional Information (per serving):
Cal: 80 | Carbs: 7g | Pro: 7g | Fat: 3g | Sugars: 4g | Fiber: 1g | Sodium: 40mg

19. Olive Focaccia Slices

Preparation time: 15 minutes
Servings: 2

Ingredients:

- 4 slices whole grain focaccia bread
- 1/4 cup chopped Kalamata olives
- 1 tablespoon extra virgin olive oil
- 1/2 teaspoon dried oregano
- 1/4 teaspoon garlic powder

Instructions:

1. Preheat the oven to 375°F (190°C).
2. Place the slices of whole grain focaccia bread on a baking sheet.

3. In a bowl, mix chopped Kalamata olives, extra virgin olive oil, dried oregano, and garlic powder.
4. Spread the olive mixture evenly over the focaccia slices.
5. Bake in the preheated oven for about 10 minutes, or until the bread is toasted and the olives are fragrant.
6. Serve the olive focaccia slices as a flavorful appetizer.

Nutritional Information (per serving):
Cal: 140 | Carbs: 22g | Pro: 4g | Fat: 5g | Sugars: 1g | Fiber: 4g | Sodium: 250mg

20. Marinated Olives Platter

Preparation time: 10 minutes
Servings: 2

Ingredients:

- 1 cup mixed olives (Kalamata, green, black, etc.)
- 1 tablespoon extra virgin olive oil
- 1 teaspoon chopped fresh rosemary
- 1 teaspoon chopped fresh thyme
- 1/2 teaspoon lemon zest
- Crushed red pepper flakes, to taste

Instructions:

1. In a bowl, toss the mixed olives with extra virgin olive oil, chopped fresh rosemary, chopped fresh thyme, lemon zest, and crushed red pepper flakes.
2. Let the olives marinate for at least 15 minutes, stirring occasionally.
3. Arrange the marinated olives on a serving platter.
4. Serve the marinated olives with whole grain crackers or bread.

Nutritional Information (per serving):
Cal: 80 | Carbs: 4g | Pro: 1g | Fat: 7g | Sugars: 0g | Fiber: 2g | Sodium: 450mg

Desserts

1. Fruity Yogurt Parfait

Preparation time: 10 minutes
Servings: 2

Ingredients:

- 1 cup Greek yogurt
- 1 cup mixed berries (blueberries, strawberries, raspberries)
- 2 tablespoons chopped nuts (walnuts, almonds)
- 1 teaspoon honey
- 1/2 teaspoon vanilla extract
- Fresh mint leaves for garnish

Instructions:

1. In each serving glass, layer 1/4 cup Greek yogurt.
2. Add a layer of mixed berries on top of the yogurt.
3. Sprinkle chopped nuts over the berries.
4. Drizzle half of the honey and vanilla extract over the nuts.
5. Repeat the layers one more time in each glass.
6. Garnish with fresh mint leaves.
7. Serve the fruity yogurt parfait as a delightful and refreshing dessert.

Nutritional Information (per serving):
Cal: 180 | Carbs: 18g | Pro: 10g | Fat: 7g | Sugars: 12g | Fiber: 4g | Sodium: 60mg

2. Almond Orange Biscotti

Preparation time: 15 minutes
Cook time: 25 minutes
Servings: 2

Ingredients:

- 1/2 cup almond flour
- 1/4 cup erythritol (or preferred sweetener)
- 1/2 teaspoon baking powder
- Zest of 1 orange
- 1 egg
- 1 teaspoon vanilla extract
- 1/4 cup chopped almonds

Instructions:

1. Preheat the oven to 325°F (165°C) and line a baking sheet with parchment paper.
2. In a bowl, mix almond flour, erythritol, baking powder, and orange zest.
3. Add the egg and vanilla extract to the dry ingredients. Mix until a dough forms.
4. Fold in chopped almonds.
5. Shape the dough into a log on the prepared baking sheet.
6. Bake for about 20-25 minutes until firm and golden.

7. Let the log cool slightly, then slice into biscotti.
8. Return the slices to the oven for an additional 5-7 minutes to crisp up.
9. Serve the almond orange biscotti with a cup of herbal tea or coffee.

Nutritional Information (per serving):
Cal: 220 | Carbs: 8g | Pro: 8g | Fat: 18g | Sugars: 1g | Fiber: 4g | Sodium: 80mg

3. Greek Yogurt Popsicles

Preparation time: 10 minutes
Cook time: 4 hours
Servings: 2

Ingredients:

- 1 cup Greek yogurt
- 1/2 cup mixed berries (blueberries, strawberries, raspberries)
- 1 tablespoon honey
- 1/2 teaspoon vanilla extract

Instructions:

1. In a bowl, mix Greek yogurt, honey, and vanilla extract until smooth.
2. Gently fold in mixed berries.
3. Pour the mixture into popsicle molds.
4. Insert popsicle sticks and freeze for at least 4 hours.
5. Remove from molds and enjoy these creamy and fruity Greek yogurt popsicles.

Nutritional Information (per serving):
Cal: 150 | Carbs: 15g | Pro: 8g | Fat: 7g | Sugars: 11g | Fiber: 2g | Sodium: 50mg

4. Berry Chia Pudding

Preparation time: 10 minutes
Cook time: 2 hours or overnight
Servings: 2

Ingredients:

- 1/4 cup chia seeds
- 1 cup unsweetened almond milk
- 1/2 cup mixed berries (blueberries, strawberries, raspberries)
- 1 tablespoon honey
- 1/2 teaspoon vanilla extract

Instructions:

1. In a bowl, mix chia seeds and almond milk.
2. Add honey and vanilla extract, and stir well.
3. Let the mixture sit for 10 minutes, then stir again to prevent clumping.

4. Cover and refrigerate for at least 2 hours or overnight.
5. Before serving, layer chia pudding and mixed berries in serving glasses.
6. Drizzle honey on top if desired.
7. Enjoy the nutrient-rich and satisfying berry chia pudding.

Nutritional Information (per serving):
Cal: 160 | Carbs: 18g | Pro: 4g | Fat: 8g | Sugars: 9g | Fiber: 10g | Sodium: 80mg

5. Roasted Fig Delight

Preparation time: 5 minutes
Cook time: 15 minutes
Servings: 2

Ingredients:

- 4 fresh figs, halved
- 1 tablespoon honey
- 2 tablespoons chopped walnuts
- 1/2 teaspoon cinnamon
- Greek yogurt for serving

Instructions:

1. Preheat the oven to 350°F (175°C) and line a baking sheet with parchment paper.
2. Place fig halves on the baking sheet, cut side up.
3. Drizzle honey over the figs and sprinkle with chopped walnuts and cinnamon.
4. Roast for about 15 minutes until figs are soft and caramelized.
5. Serve the roasted figs warm with a dollop of Greek yogurt.

Nutritional Information (per serving):
Cal: 170 | Carbs: 24g | Pro: 3g | Fat: 8g | Sugars: 19g | Fiber: 4g | Sodium: 5mg

6. Dark Chocolate Dipped Strawberries

Preparation time: 10 minutes
Cook time: 15 minutes
Servings: 2

Ingredients:

- 12 fresh strawberries, washed and dried
- 2 oz dark chocolate (70% cocoa or higher)
- 1 teaspoon coconut oil
- Chopped nuts for garnish (optional)

Instructions:

1. Line a baking sheet with parchment paper.
2. In a microwave-safe bowl, melt dark chocolate and coconut oil in 20-second intervals, stirring until smooth.
3. Dip each strawberry into the melted chocolate, allowing excess to drip off.
4. Place dipped strawberries on the prepared baking sheet.
5. If using, sprinkle chopped nuts on the chocolate before it sets.
6. Chill in the refrigerator for about 15 minutes to set the chocolate.
7. Serve the dark chocolate-dipped strawberries as a delightful and guilt-free treat.

Nutritional Information (per serving):
Cal: 130 | Carbs: 15g | Pro: 2g | Fat: 8g | Sugars: 10g | Fiber: 3g | Sodium: 0mg

7. Honeyed Almond Bites

Preparation time: 10 minutes
Cook time: 30 minutes
Servings: 2

Ingredients:

- 1/2 cup almonds
- 1 tablespoon honey
- 1/2 teaspoon cinnamon
- Pinch of sea salt

Instructions:

1. In a food processor, pulse almonds until finely chopped.
2. Add honey, cinnamon, and a pinch of sea salt. Pulse to combine.
3. Roll the mixture into small bites and place on a plate lined with parchment paper.
4. Chill the almond bites in the refrigerator for about 30 minutes.
5. Serve the honeyed almond bites as a naturally sweet and crunchy treat.

Nutritional Information (per serving):
Cal: 170 | Carbs: 11g | Pro: 5g | Fat: 13g | Sugars: 8g | Fiber: 3g | Sodium: 70mg

8. Lemon Ricotta Tartlets

Preparation time: 15 minutes
Cook time: 20 minutes
Servings: 2

Ingredients:

- 4 small whole wheat tartlet shells
- 1/2 cup ricotta cheese
- Zest of 1 lemon
- 2 tablespoons honey
- Fresh berries for topping

Instructions:

1. Preheat the oven according to the tartlet shell package instructions.
2. In a bowl, mix ricotta cheese, lemon zest, and honey until smooth.
3. Fill each tartlet shell with the ricotta mixture.
4. Bake for about 20 minutes or until tartlet shells are golden.
5. Let the tartlets cool slightly before topping with fresh berries.
6. Serve the lemon ricotta tartlets as a light and tangy dessert.

Nutritional Information (per serving):
Cal: 240 | Carbs: 26g | Pro: 8g | Fat: 12g | Sugars: 18g | Fiber: 2g | Sodium: 160mg

9. Pistachio Date Balls

Preparation time: 15 minutes
Cook time: 30 minutes
Servings: 2

Ingredients:

- 1/2 cup pitted dates
- 1/4 cup unsalted pistachios
- 1 tablespoon unsweetened shredded coconut
- 1/2 teaspoon vanilla extract
- Pinch of sea salt

Instructions:

1. In a food processor, pulse pitted dates until they form a sticky paste.
2. Add pistachios, shredded coconut, vanilla extract, and a pinch of sea salt.
3. Pulse until ingredients are combined and form a dough.
4. Roll the mixture into small balls and place on a plate lined with parchment paper.
5. Chill the pistachio date balls in the refrigerator for about 30 minutes.
6. Serve these energy-packed bites as a naturally sweet and satisfying dessert.

Nutritional Information (per serving):
Cal: 220 | Carbs: 35g | Pro: 4g | Fat: 9g | Sugars: 26g | Fiber: 4g | Sodium: 40mg

10. Baked Apple Slices

Preparation time: 10 minutes
Cook time: 20 minutes
Servings: 2

Ingredients:

- 2 small apples, cored and sliced

- 1 tablespoon honey
- 1/2 teaspoon cinnamon
- 1 tablespoon chopped walnuts
- Greek yogurt for serving

Instructions:

1. Preheat the oven to 350°F (175°C) and line a baking sheet with parchment paper.
2. In a bowl, toss apple slices with honey and cinnamon until coated.
3. Arrange the apple slices on the baking sheet in a single layer.
4. Sprinkle chopped walnuts over the apples.
5. Bake for about 20 minutes or until apples are tender.
6. Serve the baked apple slices warm with a dollop of Greek yogurt.

Nutritional Information (per serving):
Cal: 180 | Carbs: 40g | Pro: 1g | Fat: 2g | Sugars: 33g | Fiber: 6g | Sodium: 10mg

11. Coconut Rice Pudding

Preparation time: 5 minutes
Cook time: 25 minutes
Servings: 2

Ingredients:

- 1/2 cup Arborio rice
- 2 cups unsweetened coconut milk
- 2 tablespoons honey
- 1/4 teaspoon vanilla extract
- Unsweetened shredded coconut for topping

Instructions:

1. In a saucepan, combine Arborio rice and coconut milk.
2. Bring to a simmer over medium heat, then reduce to low and cover.
3. Cook for about 20-25 minutes, stirring occasionally, until rice is tender and creamy.
4. Stir in honey and vanilla extract.
5. Serve the coconut rice pudding warm or chilled, topped with a sprinkle of shredded coconut.

Nutritional Information (per serving):
Cal: 270 | Carbs: 44g | Pro: 2g | Fat: 10g | Sugars: 16g | Fiber: 1g | Sodium: 20mg

12. Watermelon Mint Sorbet

Preparation time: 10 minutes
Cook time: 4 hours
Servings: 2

Ingredients:

- 2 cups diced watermelon, seeds removed
- 1 tablespoon fresh lime juice
- 2 tablespoons chopped fresh mint
- 1 tablespoon honey (optional)

Instructions:

1. In a blender, puree diced watermelon until smooth.
2. Add lime juice and chopped mint, and blend again.
3. Taste and add honey if desired for added sweetness.
4. Pour the mixture into a shallow dish and freeze for about 4 hours, stirring occasionally.
5. Serve the watermelon mint sorbet as a refreshing and naturally sweet treat.

Nutritional Information (per serving):
Cal: 70 | Carbs: 18g | Pro: 1g | Fat: 0g | Sugars: 14g | Fiber: 1g | Sodium: 0mg

13. Greek Yogurt Mousse

Preparation time: 10 minutes
Cook time: 1 hour
Servings: 2

Ingredients:

- 1 cup Greek yogurt
- 2 tablespoons honey
- 1 teaspoon vanilla extract
- Fresh berries for topping

Instructions:

1. In a bowl, mix Greek yogurt, honey, and vanilla extract until smooth.
2. Divide the mixture between serving glasses.
3. Chill the glasses in the refrigerator for about 1 hour.
4. Before serving, top the Greek yogurt mousse with fresh berries.
5. Enjoy this light and creamy dessert with a hint of tanginess.

Nutritional Information (per serving):
Cal: 180 | Carbs: 27g | Pro: 12g | Fat: 4g | Sugars: 25g | Fiber: 1g | Sodium: 55mg

14. Orange Olive Oil Cake

Preparation time: 15 minutes
Cook time: 30 minutes
Servings: 2

Ingredients:

- 1/2 cup almond flour
- 1/4 cup whole wheat flour
- 1/4 cup erythritol (or preferred sweetener)
- Zest of 1 orange
- 1/4 cup fresh orange juice
- 2 tablespoons extra virgin olive oil
- 1 egg

Instructions:

1. Preheat the oven to 350°F (175°C) and grease two small cake pans.
2. In a bowl, mix almond flour, whole wheat flour, erythritol, and orange zest.
3. In a separate bowl, whisk together fresh orange juice, olive oil, and egg.
4. Combine the wet and dry ingredients, stirring until well combined.
5. Divide the batter between the cake pans and smooth the tops.
6. Bake for about 25-30 minutes or until a toothpick comes out clean.
7. Let the cakes cool before serving.

Nutritional Information (per serving):
Cal: 250 | Carbs: 18g | Pro: 8g | Fat: 18g | Sugars: 6g | Fiber: 4g | Sodium: 30mg

15. Mixed Berry Crumble

Preparation time: 10 minutes
Cook time: 25 minutes
Servings: 2

Ingredients:

- 2 cups mixed berries (blueberries, strawberries, raspberries)
- 1 tablespoon honey
- 1/2 teaspoon lemon juice
- 1/4 cup rolled oats
- 2 tablespoons almond flour
- 1 tablespoon chopped almonds
- 1 tablespoon coconut oil

Instructions:

1. Preheat the oven to 350°F (175°C) and grease a baking dish.
2. In a bowl, mix mixed berries, honey, and lemon juice.
3. In a separate bowl, combine rolled oats, almond flour, chopped almonds, and coconut oil.
4. Spread the berry mixture evenly in the baking dish.
5. Sprinkle the oat-almond mixture over the berries.
6. Bake for about 25 minutes or until the crumble is golden and the berries are bubbly.
7. Serve the mixed berry crumble warm with a dollop of Greek yogurt if desired.

Nutritional Information (per serving):
Cal: 210 | Carbs: 30g | Pro: 4g | Fat: 9g | Sugars: 18g | Fiber: 6g | Sodium: 5mg

16. Apricot Walnut Bars

Preparation time: 15 minutes
Cook time: 25 minutes
Servings: 2

Ingredients:

- 1/2 cup whole wheat flour
- 1/4 cup chopped dried apricots
- 1/4 cup chopped walnuts
- 2 tablespoons honey
- 1/4 teaspoon vanilla extract
- Pinch of sea salt

Instructions:

1. Preheat the oven to 350°F (175°C) and line a baking pan with parchment paper.
2. In a bowl, mix whole wheat flour, chopped apricots, and chopped walnuts.
3. In a separate bowl, whisk together honey, vanilla extract, and a pinch of sea salt.
4. Combine the wet and dry ingredients, stirring until a crumbly dough forms.
5. Press the dough into the prepared baking pan.
6. Bake for about 20-25 minutes or until golden.
7. Let the bars cool before slicing.

Nutritional Information (per serving):
Cal: 210 | Carbs: 36g | Pro: 4g | Fat: 7g | Sugars: 17g | Fiber: 4g | Sodium: 5mg

17. Chocolate Avocado Mousse

Preparation time: 10 minutes
Cook time: 1 hour
Servings: 2

Ingredients:

- 1 ripe avocado, peeled and pitted
- 2 tablespoons unsweetened cocoa powder
- 2 tablespoons honey
- 1/2 teaspoon vanilla extract
- Fresh berries for topping

Instructions:

1. In a food processor, blend avocado, cocoa powder, honey, and vanilla extract until smooth.
2. Divide the chocolate avocado mousse between serving glasses.
3. Chill the glasses in the refrigerator for about 1 hour.
4. Before serving, top the mousse with fresh berries.

5. Enjoy this rich and creamy chocolate dessert with a healthy twist.

Nutritional Information (per serving):
Cal: 230 | Carbs: 28g | Pro: 3g | Fat: 14g | Sugars: 19g | Fiber: 7g | Sodium: 10mg

18. Walnut Stuffed Dates

Preparation time: 10 minutes
Servings: 2

Ingredients:

- 8 Medjool dates, pitted
- 16 walnut halves
- 1/2 teaspoon ground cinnamon
- Pinch of sea salt

Instructions:

1. In each date, insert a walnut half.
2. Arrange the stuffed dates on a plate.
3. Sprinkle ground cinnamon and a pinch of sea salt over the dates.
4. Serve the walnut stuffed dates as a simple and naturally sweet dessert.

Nutritional Information (per serving):
Cal: 190 | Carbs: 36g | Pro: 2g | Fat: 6g | Sugars: 31g | Fiber: 4g | Sodium: 0mg

19. Pomegranate Frozen Yogurt

Preparation time: 5 minutes
Cook time: 4 hours or overnight
Servings: 2

Ingredients:

- 2 cups Greek yogurt
- 1/2 cup pomegranate arils
- 2 tablespoons honey
- 1/2 teaspoon vanilla extract

Instructions:

1. In a bowl, mix Greek yogurt, pomegranate arils, honey, and vanilla extract.
2. Pour the mixture into a shallow dish.
3. Cover and freeze for at least 4 hours or overnight, stirring occasionally.
4. Before serving, let the frozen yogurt soften slightly at room temperature.
5. Scoop the pomegranate frozen yogurt into bowls.

Nutritional Information (per serving):
Cal: 240 | Carbs: 28g | Pro: 20g | Fat: 6g | Sugars: 25g | Fiber: 1g | Sodium: 70mg

20. Cinnamon Baked Pears

Preparation time: 10 minutes
Cook time: 25 minutes
Servings: 2

Ingredients:

- 2 ripe pears, halved and cored
- 2 tablespoons chopped walnuts
- 2 tablespoons honey
- 1/2 teaspoon ground cinnamon
- Greek yogurt for serving

Instructions:

1. Preheat the oven to 350°F (175°C) and line a baking dish with parchment paper.
2. Place pear halves in the baking dish, cut side up.
3. In a bowl, mix chopped walnuts, honey, and ground cinnamon.
4. Fill the center of each pear half with the walnut mixture.
5. Bake for about 20-25 minutes or until pears are tender.
6. Serve the cinnamon baked pears warm with a dollop of Greek yogurt.

Nutritional Information (per serving):
Cal: 200 | Carbs: 46g | Pro: 2g | Fat: 4g | Sugars: 34g | Fiber: 7g | Sodium: 5mg

Meal Plan

DAY	BREAKFAST	LUNCH	DINNER
1	Berry Parfait Delight	Greek Feta Penne	Grilled Salmon Skewers
2	Spinach Omelet Roll	Mediterranean Lentil Fusilli	Lemon Herb Chicken
3	Almond Chia Pudding	Tomato Basil Linguine	Mediterranean Stuffed Peppers
4	Whole Grain Pancakes	Chickpea Pasta Primavera	Balsamic Glazed Pork
5	Avocado Toast Feast	Greek Yogurt Marinade	Shrimp and Orzo Salad
6	Mediterranean Frittata	Lemon Thyme Turkey	Herb Crusted Whitefish
7	Veggie Breakfast Wrap	Greek Lemon Chicken	Greek Turkey Burgers
8	Smoked Salmon Plate	Olive Rosemary Roast Hen	Lentil Spinach Curry
9	Quinoa Breakfast Bowl	Mediterranean Pesto Chicken	Tomato Basil Cod
10	Tomato Basil Scramble	Mediterranean Tofu Stir-fry	Chickpea Spinach Stew
11	Cottage Cheese Delight	Roasted Red Pepper Penne	Olive Roasted Chicken
12	Olive Tapenade Toast	Lemon Garlic Angel Hair	Feta Crusted Salmon
13	Mixed Berry Smoothie	Broccoli Walnut Rigatoni	Spinach Mushroom Frittata
14	Egg and Spinach Muffins	Zesty Shrimp Linguine	Greek Yogurt Marinated Chicken
15	Oatmeal Banana Bowl	Feta Arugula Farfalle	Baked Cod with Tomatoes
16	Tofu Scramble Plate	Caprese Pesto Cavatappi	Lemony Garlic Shrimp
17	Mediterranean Shakshuka	Lemon Roasted Veggies	Herb Grilled Steak
18	Almond Butter Waffles	Hummus Trio	Greek Chickpea Salad
19	Walnut Raisin Porridge	Olive Tapenade	Spinach Mushroom Risotto
20	Greek Yogurt Bowl	Quinoa Tabbouleh	Citrus Marinated Swordfish
21	Avocado Toast Feast	Garlic Spinach Saute	Greek Souvlaki Chicken
22	Berry Parfait Delight	Tomato Cucumber Salad	Tomato Basil Beef
23	Spinach Omelet Roll	Mediterranean Rice Pilaf	Orange Glazed Pork
24	Almond Chia Pudding	Roasted Red Onions	Greek Style Burgers
25	Whole Grain Pancakes	Greek Yogurt Dip	Lemon Herb Chicken
26	Veggie Breakfast Wrap	Balsamic Grilled Asparagus	Tuna Olive Orecchiette
27	Smoked Salmon Plate	Chickpea Cucumber Salad	Roasted Red Pepper
28	Mediterranean Frittata	Artichoke Hearts Saute	Tofu Scramble Plate
29	Quinoa Breakfast Bowl	Roasted Brussels Sprouts	Zesty Shrimp Linguine
30	Tomato Basil Scramble	Greek Salad	Spinach Mushroom Frittata
31	Cottage Cheese Delight	Lemon Garlic Angel Hair	Feta Crusted Salmon

DAY	BREAKFAST	LUNCH	DINNER
32	Olive Tapenade Toast	Broccoli Walnut Rigatoni	Greek Yogurt Marinated Chicken
33	Mixed Berry Smoothie	Spinach Feta Stuffed Mushrooms	Baked Cod with Tomatoes
34	Egg and Spinach Muffins	Caprese Skewers	Lemony Garlic Shrimp
35	Oatmeal Banana Bowl	Roasted Garlic Cauliflower	Herb Grilled Steak
36	Tofu Scramble Plate	Mediterranean Zucchini Pasta	Greek Chickpea Salad
37	Mediterranean Shakshuka	Lemon Herb Orzo Soup	Citrus Marinated Swordfish
38	Almond Butter Waffles	Tomato Basil Linguine	Greek Souvlaki Chicken
39	Walnut Raisin Porridge	Greek Feta Penne	Lemon Herb Chicken
40	Greek Yogurt Bowl	Chickpea Pasta Primavera	Mediterranean Stuffed Peppers
41	Avocado Toast Feast	Garlic Spinach Spaghetti	Balsamic Glazed Pork
42	Berry Parfait Delight	Hummus Trio	Shrimp and Orzo Salad
43	Spinach Omelet Roll	Olive Tapenade	Herb Crusted Whitefish
44	Almond Chia Pudding	Roasted Red Onions	Greek Turkey Burgers
45	Whole Grain Pancakes	Greek Yogurt Dip	Lentil Spinach Curry
46	Veggie Breakfast Wrap	Tomato Cucumber Salad	Tomato Basil Cod
47	Smoked Salmon Plate	Artichoke Hearts Saute	Chickpea Spinach Stew
48	Mediterranean Frittata	Lemon Roasted Veggies	Tuna Olive Orecchiette
49	Quinoa Breakfast Bowl	Roasted Brussels Sprouts	Olive Roasted Chicken
50	Tomato Basil Scramble	Spinach Feta Stuffed Mushrooms	Feta Crusted Salmon
51	Cottage Cheese Delight	Mediterranean Zucchini Pasta	Greek Yogurt Marinated Chicken
52	Olive Tapenade Toast	Lemon Herb Orzo Soup	Lemony Garlic Shrimp
53	Mixed Berry Smoothie	Garlic Spinach Spaghetti	Herb Grilled Steak
54	Egg and Spinach Muffins	Greek Feta Penne	Greek Chickpea Salad
55	Oatmeal Banana Bowl	Chickpea Pasta Primavera	Citrus Marinated Swordfish
56	Tofu Scramble Plate	Tomato Basil Linguine	Greek Souvlaki Chicken
57	Mediterranean Shakshuka	Hummus Trio	Lemon Herb Chicken
58	Almond Butter Waffles	Olive Tapenade	Mediterranean Stuffed Peppers
59	Walnut Raisin Porridge	Artichoke Hearts Saute	Balsamic Glazed Pork
60	Greek Yogurt Bowl	Roasted Red Onions	Shrimp and Orzo Salad

Conversion Tables

VOLUME EQUIVALENTS (DRY)

US STANDARD	METRIC (APPROXIMATE)
1/8 Teaspoon	0.5 ml
1/4 Teaspoon	1 ml
1/2 Teaspoon	2 ml
3/4 Teaspoon	4 ml
1 Teaspoon	5 ml
1 Tablespoon	15 ml
1/4 Cup	59 ml
1/2 Cup	118 ml
3/4 Cup	177 ml
1 Cup	235 ml
2 Cups	475 ml
3 Cups	700 ml
4 Cups	1 l

WEIGHT EQUIVALENTS

US STANDARD	METRIC (APPROXIMATE)
1 Ounce	28 g
2 Ounces	57 g
5 Ounces	142 g
10 Ounces	284 g
15 Ounces	425 g
16 Ounces (1 Pound)	455g
1.5 Pounds	680 g
2 Pounds	907 g

TEMPERATURES EQUIVALENTS

FAHRENHEIT (F)	CELSIUS (C) (APPROXIMATE)
225 °F	107 °C
250 °F	120 °C
275 °F	135 °C
300 °F	150 °C
325 °F	160 °C
350 °F	180 °C
375 °F	190 °C
400 °F	205 °C
425 °F	220 °C
450 °F	235 °C
475 °F	245 °C
500 °F	260 °C

VOLUME EQUIVALENTS (LIQUID)

US STANDARD	US STANDARD (OUNCES)	METRIC (APPROXIMATE)
2 Tablespoons	1 fl.oz.	30 ml
1/4 Cup	2 fl.oz.	60 ml
1/2 Cup	4 fl.oz.	120 ml
1 Cup	8 fl.oz.	240 ml
1 1/2 Cups	12 fl.oz.	355 ml
2 Cups or 1 Pint	16 fl.oz.	475 ml
4 Cups or 1 Quart	32 fl.oz.	1 l
1 Gallon	128 fl.oz.	4 l

Bonus

As I promised, here are the directions to download the 2 Bonuses:

HEART HEALTHY COOKBOOK FOR BEGINNERS
Complement your Mediterranean culinary adventure with our exclusive bonus, the "Heart Healthy Cookbook for Beginners." Packed with flavorful recipes designed to promote heart health, this bonus is a valuable addition to your wellness journey. From nutrient-rich salads to delectable lean protein dishes, this cookbook guides you through creating delicious meals that love your heart as much as your taste buds do.

DASH DIET COOKBOOK FOR BEGINNERS
As a special bonus, we're including the "DASH Diet Cookbook for Beginners." Discover the powerful Dietary Approaches to Stop Hypertension (DASH) principles and embark on a path to lower blood pressure and improved health.
With recipes focused on reducing sodium while maximizing taste, this bonus empowers you to embrace a dietary approach that's backed by science and crafted for your well-being.

How to download your Bonueses?

Easy! Scan this QR Code and follow the directions on the Web page!

I really hope you enjoyed this book and will find 1 minute to
leave me a honest review on Amazon.

If you found any errors or inconsistencies, please contact me.
My readers' feedback is very important to me and I do everything
I can to ensure you and everyone has the best reading experience.